WITH OR WITHOUT YOU

WITH OR WITHOUT YOU

A MEMOIR

DOMENICA RUTA

SPIEGEL & GRAU | NEW YORK

This is a work of nonfiction. Some names and
identifying details have been changed.

Published in the United States by Spiegel & Grau,
an imprint of The Random House Publishing Group,
a division of Random House, Inc., New York.

SPIEGEL & GRAU and design is a
registered trademark of Random House, Inc.

LIBRARY OF CONGRESS CATALOGING-IN-PUBLICATION DATA

Ruta, Domenica.
With or without you : a memoir / Domenica Ruta.
p. cm.
ISBN 978-0-8129-9324-0
eBook ISBN 978-0-679-64502-3
1. Children of drug addicts—Massachusetts—Biography.
2. Drug addicts—Massachusetts—Biography. I. Title.
HV5831.M4R88 2013
362.29'13092—dc23
[B] 2012017991

Printed in the United States of America on acid-free paper

www.spiegelandgrau.com

2 4 6 8 9 7 5 3

Book design by Barbara M. Bachman

For her

YOU WERE SICK, BUT NOW YOU'RE WELL,
AND THERE'S WORK TO DO.

—*Kurt Vonnegut*

WITH OR
WITHOUT YOU

Glass

———————

MY MOTHER GRABBED THE IRON POKER FROM THE FIREPLACE and said, "Get in the car."

I pulled on my sneakers and followed her outside. She had that look on her face, distracted and mean, as though she'd just been dragged out of a deep sleep full of dreams. She was mad, I could tell right away, but not at me, not this time.

Her car was a lime-green hatchback with blotches and stripes of putty smeared over the dents. The Shitbox, she called it. *We* called it, actually. My mother hated the thing so much she didn't mind if I swore at it. "What a piece of shit," I'd grumble whenever it stalled on us, which we could gamble on happening at least once a day, more if it was snowing. Far and away the most unreliable car we ever had in our life together, it was a machine that ran on prayer.

Among the car's many other defects, the inside casing of the passenger door had broken off, leaving the mechanical skeleton that controlled the window and lock exposed. I poked my fingers inside the levers, watching the sinewy rubber push and pull, the metal joints grasp and release. A spectacular display. I couldn't get enough of it.

"Stop it," Mum said. She reached over and grabbed my hand. "This car's old as me." More than twenty years, at least. "I don't know how much longer it's going to stay in one piece."

"Where are we going?" I asked her.

She lit the cigarette bobbing anxiously between her lips and slid her key into the ignition. I held my breath. It was a ritual so intuitive that I never questioned its provenance or worth, silently assuming that any exchange I might have with the present atmosphere would choke up the magic at work under the car's hood. And then what? Would we be able to drive to school, work, and stores, like everyone else in the suburbs? Or would we hear the familiar sputter and cough that so often ruined our day?

"Come on," Mum whispered. "Come on."

A rumble. The engine turned over. We were going somewhere.

My mother and I lived on the North Shore of Massachusetts. Boston was only thirty minutes away, though we seldom made it out that far. Not in one of her cars. Wherever we went that day was close to home, because we drove for only a few minutes before she parked on a quiet, tree-lined street and got out. I remember watching her body pass by through the windshield, then jumping into her arms as she opened the door, lifted me up, and sat me on top of the car's hood. It was a cool gray day and the metal felt warm beneath my legs. Mum leaned into the open driver's-side window and pulled out our fireplace poker from the backseat. Then, without a word, she began smashing the windshield of someone else's car.

This other car was red, I remember, but it's possible I'm wrong, that over the years I've painted it in my mother's rage. How old was I? Four, maybe five? Small enough still that my mother sometimes carried me but too old to be shocked by the things she did.

My mother. Her name was Kathleen, which she shortened to Kathi. Spell it with a Y or, God forbid, a C, and she'd lacerate your face with her scowl. She was a hair taller than five feet and I once saw her turn over a refrigerator during a fight with one of her boyfriends. The core of her strength was concentrated in her lungs. Like all the women in our bloodline, Kathi was a screamer. Sometimes she opened her mouth and the screech that came out sustained for minutes without breaking or getting hoarse. She used to bend down to scream directly into my face, and I would get lost staring at the black fillings in her molars, the heat of her breath touching my skin like a finger. But volume was never an accurate herald of my mother's mood; loud was simply the who and the what of her. That voice, those big dangling earrings, the long red nails and skintight jeans and shirts slit open a few inches below the cleavage of her enormous breasts. I was forever climbing onto my mother's lap, trying to button her shirt higher. "No, Honey," she'd say, pulling my hands off her chest. "Mummy *wants* to show off her boobies right now." Her hair was almost black, but she insisted on bleaching it Deborah Harry blond. She had one tattoo, a small but regrettable crab on her left ring finger. It was her astrological sign—the Cancer. Even she was ashamed of it, I know, because she hid it under a gold wedding band long before she ever married.

What else do you need to know about this woman before I go on with the story? That she believed it was more important to be an interesting person than it was to be a good one; that she allowed me to skip school whenever I wanted to, and if there was a good movie on TV she wouldn't let me go to school because, she said, she *needed* me to stay home and watch it with her; that, thanks to this education, I was the only girl in the second grade who could recite entire scenes from *Scarface* and *The Godfather* by heart; that she made me responsible for most of my own meals when I was seven and all the laundry in the house when I was nine; that her ability to make money was alchemical; that she was vainer than a beauty queen, but the last time I saw her she weighed more than two hundred pounds and her arms were encrusted with purulent sores; that she loved me so much she couldn't help hating me; that at least once a week I still dream she is trying to kill me.

Now, where was I?

Bashing the windshield of a red car.

This car belonged to a woman named Josie, an ex-girlfriend of my mother's only brother. I don't know whether my uncle asked my mother for this favor or if she had volunteered. Either way seems plausible now. My mother's Italian-American family had a thuggish, moronic code of honor that everyone violated as often as they upheld it. This windshield job was an act of loyalty. I learned as I grew up that my mother would demand nothing less of me.

At this point in Kathi's life she weighed about a hundred and twenty-five pounds. With such a pillowy shape on her diminutive frame, the woman didn't have powerful torque on her side. But put a metal bar and some anger in her hands and Mum could swing like Ted Williams.

After what seemed a long time, the windshield chipped in one spot.

"Don't look at Mummy right now, okay?" she muttered to me.

What else was I supposed to be watching? And who was she trying to kid? My mother loved an audience. No one knew this better than I did.

She took a few more whacks and the chip began to crack outward in jagged spokes, the shape of the sun as I drew it in my crayon landscapes.

Sitting on the hood of the car, I wanted nothing more than to hear the glass shatter, but it was taking forever. My mother and I seemed to realize this at the same moment, because she stopped, turned to look at me, and shrugged, as if to say, "You'd think this would be easier."

My body leaned toward hers like a plant stretching in the direction of the sunniest window in the room. I prayed with each strike that we would finally hear it—the lovely, delicate rainfall of something whole now in pieces. My mother beat that woman's windshield with everything she had, but it would not shatter. Eventually she gave up. We got back into the car and drove home in silence, both of us longing for the sound of breaking glass.

Dirty

M Y CHILDHOOD TOOK PLACE IN THE 1980S. I CUT MY BABY TEETH
on the cardboard record sleeve of Supertramp's *Breakfast in America*. Ronald Reagan was president. Mr. Macaroni Mouth, I used to call him: I don't remember why. Kathi had a special salute whenever his dour face appeared on TV.

"Ba fungul," she said, brushing her hand under her chin. She flicked her thumb against her top front teeth, shot a middle finger into the air, pretended to spit. "He was an actor, you know. Not even a good one. Westerns. Glorified soap operas."

My mother hated Ronald Reagan so much that I assumed she knew him intimately—that he was just another of the many in a revolving door of friends she was always complaining had ripped her off. As my mother saw it, the things Reagan was saying about her were getting low-down and personal. What she meant, of course, was her demographic—the single mother on welfare. It seemed every other night there was a special feature on the evening news reviling these women, until they became the fictional antagonist of the straining American economy. Mum took things like this to heart.

There were plenty of times when Kathi was capable of performing the role of the empowered, hardworking single mother. At Christmas, for example, she would take on a second, sometimes third job as a cashier at the local toy franchise just so she could get her hands on the coveted toy of the season. One year it was a pig-faced doll with a cowlick of orange yarn, which I later abused mercilessly by beating its oversize plastic head against the sidewalk. Kathi had hidden this doll under her register so that when the mad rush was over and the store had sold out there would be one left for me, one that she could pay for on layaway.

If there was an indulgence that could be purchased, my mother would find the money for it, any extracurricular curiosity I entertained had her whipping out the checkbook so she could pay someone to nurture it. This is how I became a passionate child-dilettante of ballet, photography, oceanography, and conversational French. At some point when I was eight or nine, I connected the notes of a famous classical piece I heard in cartoons to its composer, Beethoven. Kathi was so thrilled she bought me tickets to a children's series at the Boston Symphony Orchestra. Every Saturday morning for six weeks, I rode with a troupe of young classical enthusiasts and their parents on a school bus into the city. Knowing she would never be able to wake up in time to drive me to the rendezvous point, Kathi hired a taxi to take me there and paid in advance. When I expressed an interest in computers, she waitressed at a Colonial-themed restaurant that made her wear a bonnet for the Sunday brunch shift. She worked every weekend for two months, long enough to buy me a brand-new Apple IIe, then called in sick one morning and never went back. She worked stints as a bartender, a salesgirl in a tourist attraction presiding over a lobster tank, and a canteen truck driver. This was my favorite of her jobs, though it didn't last long. I enjoyed the endless stock of Kit Kats and getting to ride in a great big truck with my mum. She did not enjoy getting up before dawn every day. I think the only reason she took that job in the first place was to go boyfriend hunting, but her prince was not to be found at a construction site.

Kathi was once inspired by an ad on TV to sign up for a course in TV/VCR repair. I remember seeing the thick hardcover textbook open on our coffee table, every single sentence ablaze with my mother's pink highlighter. A razor and a shortened straw lay on a dish nearby. I think she went to the first two classes before quitting. In a pinch Kathi would sell cocaine, but, like waiting tables, it was a temporary means to an end, never something she counted on as her primary vocation.

Then there were periods when my mother was just as happy to sleep all day and collect welfare. On the first of the month she would hop around our apartment, waving her check at me and singing, "Free Money Day! Free Money Day!" I danced at her heels, rattling off the list of toys I had been dreaming about since the dissipation of last month's check. My mother would spend every dime of her welfare check immediately on cocaine, new clothes, new coloring books and dolls, and maybe a night or two of take-out Chinese. We lived on the leftovers for as long as possible. By the end of the month we'd be fisting the couch for loose change and I'd be off to the corner store with a pocket full of quarters to buy milk, Slim Jims, and cigarettes.

The two of us lived in the basement of the house her father had built when she was in high school. She rented the one-bedroom apartment from her mother, who charged a hundred dollars a month, or whatever my mother was able to give her. Her brother lived in the big house upstairs, first with a group of single guys and later with his wife and kids, and paid the same monthly amount to his mother, who lived next door in the little ramshackle camp where the whole family had started out a generation earlier. Mum called our plot of land the Ruta Compound.

"We're just like the Kennedys," she said.

WHERE AND WHEN WE got the name Ruta I have no idea. There is no one I can safely ask, as the members of my tribe are notorious throughout the North Shore as a band of lunatics who lie even when the truth would do just as well. So I don't know when the first Rutas got on that boat to cross the Atlantic or what port bit its thumb at them in a final farewell, only that some of us hail from a blister in the boot of Italy, the rest from that rock the boot's aiming to kick out of the Adriatic, Sicily, and that all this emigrating was an old story by the time my grandmother was born.

After his tour in World War II, my grandfather bought a tiny summer cottage on a river in Danvers, Massachusetts, winterized it as cheaply as possible, and set up his family there. The street was called Eden Glen Avenue, a dead-end road surrounded on three sides by a river and a salt marsh. My mother grew up there and twenty years later, so did I.

Our home was always too hot, too cold, and too small, but worth it, my mother insisted, because when we left our windows open we could smell the tides going in and out. Out back was a field of tall, feathery reeds fringed by tidal flats of black mud. The river flowed into the Atlantic less than a mile past our house. Generations of swans nested in the marsh. Like my family, they had been living there since before I was born. Every summer a harem of seals swam down from the Arctic and piled on a floating dock in the middle of the river. My mother, grandmother, aunts, and I would all walk down to the beach at the end of Eden Glen to say hello to them, a homecoming parade that marked the official beginning of our summer. The seals lay one on top of another and sunned themselves all day long, fat and serene in their big glistening pile. For no reason I could ever discern, the whole pod would start barking at the same time. Then, just as suddenly, they would fall silent.

These animals, this river—it all belonged to us. I decided this in the way that only children and dictators assume things, by pointing a finger and saying it is so.

I WAS AFRAID OF everything in the natural and supernatural worlds and a river is the nexus of both. The waters surrounding Eden Glen were home to riptides, toxic waste, dragons, sharks, ghosts, naiads, and, in the phragmites growing up on the banks, bloodsucking Lyme ticks. Not until my teens—my late teens, really—was I brave enough to walk to the river alone. Before that I would get close to the water only if my mother or my grandmother came with me. We'd climb down the little hill to the tiny beach that surfaced at low tide. On clear summer nights, we'd cut through a path in the backyard to the small pier built by my grandfather years before. The pier was a scenic place to watch the sun set, brood, and slap mosquitoes on one another's arms. No one had the patience for fishing and, besides, you couldn't eat anything caught off Eden Glen. The river was too polluted, first by a shoe factory on another tributary a century earlier, and later by the yacht club across the channel from us. The boats were always spilling gasoline into the water, and they thought the shallow water near our house was the best place to flush their toilets. I remember the grotesque beauty of those hot summer days, when petroleum rainbows would encircle thousands of dollops of floating human shit. I would stare in stupefied wonder, as at so many mandalas rising and falling on the surface of the water.

The family that owned the yacht club lived next door to us, and for their crimes against the river my mother would spit on the ground whenever she saw them drive by. "Your baby's going to come out mongoloid for what you did to that water," she once yelled as the pregnant wife drove past our house.

"Mum!" I gasped. "Her window was down. She might have heard you."

"Good," my mother said.

The river was one of the few things in this world that Kathi felt like protecting. For a while she volunteered with local environmentalists who dispatched her to collect samples of river water in coded plastic vials. She woke before dawn and sneaked into our neighbors' yards to take photographs of the marsh grass they mowed illegally and the seawalls they weren't supposed to build. There was a lawsuit at one point, and my mother couldn't wait to take the stand.

"Maybe I'll become a lawyer," she mused.

Real-life lawsuits are utterly lacking in the drama she craved, and, like anything in Mum's care, she gave up when the fight became more work than fun.

With or without my mother's help, some official code was eventually passed, and the boats were instructed to flush their heads farther out at sea. I never dipped a toe in that water even then, no longer from fear but from spite. My mother already had so little attention to give that sharing her with anything else made me mortally pissed off. I watched that river through the windows of our house like a jilted lover studying her rival. It was the ultimate antagonist, always beautiful and never the same. Sometimes the waves licked the grass gently as a dog attending to his fur. A strong wind would later chop the water into a rhythmic progression of crests. These sudsy waves might later shrink into the tiniest ripples. Or disappear altogether, like the day I noticed that the surface of the river was as smooth as a pane of glass. I stood at the kitchen window and stared, elated and afraid. What made this happen? Would it ever happen again? What did it mean?

The Porter River, I learned it was called years and years after I left home. It was always just the River to us. Growing up, I thought that my mother was the one who called in the tides.

KATHI AND I WERE the two most outrageous snobs ever to receive public assistance. My mother had grown up middle-class and, despite the succession of menial jobs she held, she refused to let go of certain standards. No matter how broke Mum was, she would find a way to outfit me in designer clothes. The telephone was sometimes cut off for nonpayment, but you'd better believe she paid that cable bill on time. Groceries could wait another day, but Calvin Klein and HBO could not.

I remember nights when Mum would get really high and keep me up for hours, sitting on my bed and holding forth like a monarch unjustly deposed. We were not meant for this life, she would say. There were Cadillacs in our future. A summerhouse on Martha's Vineyard. I was going to grow up and marry a Kennedy, she promised. In reality she sent me to a day-care center run by Catholic Charities, where I contracted diseases only babies in Third World countries still get.

We made do with what we had, and for what we lacked we pretended. Learning our parts from our two favorite movies, *Mommie Dearest* and *Reversal of Fortune,* my mother and I would act out scenes in our tiny basement apartment, speaking in affected voices, wishing out loud that we could be the twisted, tormented millionaires who dominated our imagination. My mother was Sunny von Bülow, the bleach-blond tyrant in yet another coma, and I was her devoted maid, trying to wake her up. "My lady," I would say, brandishing a feather duster, as I stood fretfully at her bedside. She was Joan Crawford, the abusive egomaniac, and I was her tortured Christina. Mum chased me around the apartment with a clothes hanger as though she were going to beat me. I would run from her in a fit of giggles, and when I finally let her catch me, she'd pin me to the bed, the hanger raised above her head. She would bite her lower lip and bring the hanger down hard and fast, stopping herself an inch, sometimes less than an inch, above my face.

"Wire hangers!" she'd cry out. It was our favorite game.

DURING KATHI'S SEDENTARY SPELLS, which could last anywhere between a couple of days and several weeks, she lay regally in her bed consuming four or five movies in a row. My mother was both a movie slut and a film snob: she'd watch just about anything that was on, but she would press Record only if the story was truly great.

"What are you doing?" she'd call from under the covers, a smoldering ashtray always close by braiding threads of cigarette smoke in the air like a loom. "Make me some toast," she'd yell. "Don't be stingy with the butter." Soup, a fresh book of matches, some chocolate milk—these were the things I was constantly fetching for her. Then sometimes she'd bellow, "Honey! You have to watch this movie with me."

"I'm doing my homework."

"This is more important. I promise. You'll thank me later."

I watched the canon of American cinema in my mother's smoky bedroom. The two *Godfathers* were a staple, and anything and everything by Martin Scorsese. Sonny Corleone, Travis Bickle—these guys were as real to us as Zeus and Apollo were in the homes of ancient Greece. Mum was a fool for zany real-estate comedies from the forties and their remakes in the eighties. She referred to Mel Brooks as her boyfriend. But her absolute favorite was Woody Allen. We raided the local video store for every film he ever made.

"Your grandmother's grandfather was a Sicilian Jew," my mother mentioned as we watched *Annie Hall* for the thirtieth time. "It's a big family secret. Don't tell her I told you."

Who knows if that's true or not, but there was something about our lives that echoed the paradox of Jewish history: we certainly *felt* like God's chosen people, and that we had been cursed to live in exile.

"My grammy never gave gifts," Alvy Singer says to his pretty midwestern girlfriend. "She was too busy getting raped by Cossacks."

Mum and I lay in her big unmade bed, howling from the depths of our souls.

THERE WERE VERY FEW books in our house beyond the Agatha Christies I brought home from the library. The only three books I can remember my family actually owning were a cartoon book about Italian stereotypes; an illustrated compendium of—let's call it *The Variety of Flatulent Experience;* and *Diaries of Mario M. Cuomo,* the only hardcover of the three. These books circulated the bathroom floors of my mother and all her siblings for most of the 1980s, until the paper macerated to the pulp from which it came.

I was born with a wolfish appetite for the printed word. Sometime in preschool I learned how to read—the words *clam box* on a chalkboard menu at a fried-fish stand were my first, according to my father; "Nikki (hearts) Mummy," in a crayoned note, contended my mother, though both agreed on the fact that I was no bigger than four, and that reading seemed to be a skill I'd somehow picked up on my own. In an extended family where people stumbled—and stumbled *proudly*—over three-syllable words, such a drooling little fiend for literature was endearing to no one. (It should be noted that even the most illiterate of my clan knew their way around a food-stamp application, a subpoena, and a workman's compensation claim. We were nothing if not adroit at manipulating the system.) To the philistines around me, books were a form of contraband, and curiosity wasn't so much a sin as a force of nature that would eventually kill you. So I read the *Salem Evening News,* a daily paper that we bought only when someone we knew made an appearance in the police log. I read the weekly *TV Guide* that came in the mail. I read the electricity bill and learned my first Latin, *arrears.* If it had been possible to lap words off an aluminum can spilled out of a dumpster, I would shamelessly have gotten down on all fours.

Hunger like this is pitiful. It never affords you the luxury of distinguishing between useless and important knowledge, between good and bad words. And, like movies, bad words were another resource in which my family was truly rich.

GROWING UP, MY COUSINS and I were inseparable, all of us shuffling back and forth to one another's houses every weekend. My mother and her sister Penny were the closest in age, and they both had daughters about two years apart, so it was ordained that this cousin and I would be best friends. On the day that Penny brought her baby home from the hospital, I had impetigo and my mouth was covered with contagious red sores. My mother made me stand in the far corner of the room, where I watched all the aunts gather around the bassinet to ooh and aah. It was clear that I wasn't going to get a turn to hold the new baby, so I cried and cried, my arms reaching out to her. "Fafa, Fafa!" I whimpered, because I was too small to pronounce my cousin's name. This gave rise to a lot of ridiculous diminutives. Fafa is the least nauseating, so that's what we'll call her here.

My cousin lived with her mother and stepfather in an apartment on Interstate Route 95, behind a little commercial strip that included a tattoo parlor and a pawnshop. There was a nuclear power plant not far away. For fun, Fafa liked to ride her bike to the plant and throw rocks against the chain-link fence that guarded it. I would wheeze behind her on a scooter, whining all the way, "Can we *please* go home now?"

I found out later that she was lying, that the fence enclosed nothing more than an empty lot. Fafa was cunning. You had to respect that about her. She knew that I'd been traumatized by the news stories of Chernobyl. She'd seen me crying, practically hyperventilating, about the threat of nuclear holocaust to our grandmother, whose soothing words I will never forget:

"What are you crying about, Nikki? If a nuclear power plant blows, we'll all be nothing but fucking molecules. The whole human race is like a fart in the universe. *Pllppllff,* we're here. *Pllppllff,* we're gone."

My cousin had the fearlessness of a little kid who's too cute to get into any real trouble. She slept soundly in a bedroom with posters of Freddy Krueger and Hulk Hogan on every wall. I would lie in a sleeping bag on the floor, my eyes moving from the cold Aryan glare of the Hulk to the raw-hamburger flesh of Freddy Krueger's face, and as soon as I shut my eyes my mind flooded with scenes of nuclear winter. The power plant was going to blow, I was sure of it, and probably on a weekend when I was sleeping over. As my cousin murmured softly in her sleep, I could hear the hollow, rhythmic bleating of an air raid. Outside, the highways were gridlocked with crashed cars. Trees turned to columns of ash before my very eyes. Even if I survived (doubtful with Aunt Penny in charge), the radiation poisoning would make all my hair fall out. No, I decided bravely on my cousin's bedroom floor, I'd be lucky to be in the eye of the storm when it happened; I would rather die than go bald.

Fafa was an exquisite child. I was not. I had a wrinkled forehead and perpetual dark circles around my eyes, as though I were staying up all night grinding out coke-fueled solutions to the world's problems. With my black, bushy unibrow, the faint scribble of a mustache on my upper lip, and my greasy, unbrushed hair, I looked like the bastard child of Frida Kahlo and Martin Scorsese. Fafa had a cute upturned nose, rosy cheeks, and dark brown eyes that shone like gem-polished stones. Her voice was sweet and got adorably squeaky when she talked about something she loved, like the World Wrestling Federation or the *Nightmare on Elm Street* franchise.

Watching TV with my cousin became a primer in the art of war.

We were supposed to take turns, hour for hour, even stephen, but the only way she could get me to watch her wrestling or horror shows was to broker a deal. New Year's Eve 1990, she dared me to watch a marathon of all three of *The Exorcist* movies. Our contract, which we put in writing, declared that if I stayed awake for all three movies and didn't cry I got to pick every movie we watched for the entire month of January. As this included a whole week of school vacation, I thought it was more than generous.

A brilliant scam, I can see in hindsight. Fafa was the size of a peanut, but she kicked my ass thoroughly every time we fought. She was the uncontestable victor long before midnight, when I passed out during the opening credits of the first sequel, my pillow soaked with tears.

I had one trump card, though, and I used it liberally. All I had to do was look my cousin in the eye and say, "Wrestling is fake, you know."

Fafa would explode with tears of rage and willful disbelief. "You're such a lying whore!"

Whore was one of the first swearwords I learned, a noun applicable as both an insult and a term of endearment in our family: "What are you whores up to this weekend?" "Son of a whore, I forgot my wallet at home!" Truly manifold in its application, sometimes *whore* simply meant "female." Often it was used to denote something difficult or obstinate. For example, when struggling to open a tightly screwed jar of olives, my mother might utter, "What a little whore." It had nothing to do with sex or money, unless, arriving at the bank just as the doors were locked, my grandmother would shake her fists at the whores inside.

Like a saturnine dialect of Yiddish-cum-Latin, Italian swearwords were a lot safer than their English counterparts, in part because of their obscurity, but more so for the droll linguistic entanglements your mouth is forced to make while pronouncing them. *Buchiach! Schoocci a mentz! Minchia! Incazzato!* Precise translation issues abound, but who cares when a word is so much fun to say? Sicilian, and my grandmother's peasant Sicilian in particular, is pretty much untranslatable in English. It's a language composed of consonant pilings and blithe morbidity. So in our family the word for a woman who literally takes money for sex was never *whore* but *putan*. When I was five, my grandmother defined it for me as "a woman who only shops at night."

If cursing has a matriarchal order, and for the Rutas it did, then *cunt* is the Queen Mother. This was how I knew when Mum was really, really, *really* mad. She called me so many things, but this Grand Dame of words she saved for special occasions, those singular episodes of rage that carried on from sundown and well into the next day. "You cunt, you no-good cunt, you no-good miserable little cunt . . . ," she would say in a tired, malevolent hiss, like an infant having screamed herself into exhaustion. At times like these I clung to the word *little*. It suggested a seed of affection, a promise that when this mood blew over, she would love me again.

Like any of our curses, the *c*-word had multiple uses. I'll never forget the beautiful summer day when my mother dared Fafa and me to call a stranger a cunt.

"Just say it to anyone," she said. "I'll give you five dollars." We were lying on our towels at the beach. My mother had coated herself in olive oil and was holding a record cover unfolded and wrapped in aluminum foil to reflect more sun onto her face.

"Why?" I asked.

"To see what happens," she said. "To see the look on the person's face. A social experiment. Please. Just do it for me."

My mother was a creature that needed to lick her fingers and touch an open wire every once in a while. She required this kind of jolt. It was the only way she could be sure she was still alive.

I knew from experience that there were far worse things you could be called than cunt. Earlier that year, my mother and I had gone shopping at a Neiman Marcus. Mum had somehow earned a thick wad of twenties and was impatient to spend it, every last dollar, on something frivolous. None of the salesgirls at Neiman's would help us. To be fair, I don't remember them being rude. They just skated out of our way as we examined a rack of leather skirts. Kathi was insecure and often preemptively slaughtered the nearest human being to compensate for her feelings. This person was usually me, but on that particular day it was a young redhead wearing a gold nametag and too much mascara.

"Do you see this, Nikki? They won't stop watching us, like we might steal something. It's prejudice." She marched over to the redheaded clerk and shook a fistful of cash in her face. "Excuse me," my mother said. "I won't be treated like white trash by some cunt who works *retail*."

The insult there was not the expletive but that disgraceful word beginning with *r*.

Though we tossed the *c*-word around fearlessly in my family, I knew that in the outside world it was the hydrogen bomb of curses, and I was afraid to deploy it at a peaceful place like the beach.

"Mum, please, I don't want to. Okay?"

"If you don't, I will," Fafa piped up. She was eight or nine years old that summer, and was, to use my mother's phrase, a lot ballsier than I was.

A woman in a pink bikini was approaching our spot on the sand. As much as I prayed that this woman would walk by without incident, something about her seemed to beg for degradation. She swaggered past us, audaciously comfortable in her own skin, trusting in a world she believed to be civilized.

"Cunt!" Fafa said.

The woman looked back at us with a stupefied expression and almost tripped on her flip-flops. My mother laughed her loud, gull screech of a laugh. I felt my face go up in flames and covered my head with a towel. As soon as we got home from the beach, my mother got on the phone and called Penny. I remember shrinking in the dark hallway where the phone hung while she talked to Aunt Penny, her body keeling with laughter.

"Oh no, no, no," my mother said into the phone. "You know Nikki. She's so afraid of what other people think."

Later, when I started high school in a new town where no one knew me, I decided it was a good time to start over and go by my real

name, Domenica. Even though this was the name on my birth certificate and on every single legal document pertaining to my life,
Aunt Penny saw it as proof of what an élitist phony I was. She
wouldn't shut up about it.

"Hey, Nikki—oh, *excuse me,* Domenica." She rolled her eyes.

"I don't get it," I said to my mother. "It's not like I'm asking to be
called Lady Di."

I wasn't even asking my family to call me Domenica, only the
teachers and kids at my new school. Aunt Penny balked as if I'd
started wearing a monocle and affecting a British accent. That is,
when I saw her, which was becoming more seldom. Penny had sensed
a rift coming between her daughter and me, and though our growing
apart was inevitable, it was still a few years away. I was becoming
more bookish and withdrawn, Fafa more social and tame. My cousin
was two years younger than I was, but she was already submitting
herself to that ritual teen-girl change that demands hours of primp-
ing in front of a mirror.

"You're becoming *docile,*" I told my cousin. "Your friends are all
cretins."

Half of me understood what these words meant, the other half
just loved to hear myself say them. Fafa was every bit as smart as I
was, but she had picked up a new skill that would evade me for
years—how to maintain a group of friends. On weekends she pre-
ferred going to the mall with them than watching movies with me.
Later that year she stopped returning my phone calls altogether. It
was a silent dismissal, almost harrowing in its civility. Fafa and I were
our mothers' daughters—we knew how to put on a good fight—but
there were no shrieking Italian curses in our breakup, no fists full of
each other's hair. I was crushed, but my mother was the one who
cried.

"My sisters hate you," Kathi sobbed. "They've been jealous of
you since the day you were born."

I couldn't bear to see my mother in tears, so I tried my best to
comfort her. The cousins were growing up, I explained. Now that we

weren't little kids who needed to be watched, there wasn't as much reason for the family to get together anymore.

Or so we thought. Although we no longer spent every weekend together as before, our family still gathered on holidays and birthdays without inviting my mother and me.

"It's because of you," Kathi loved to say. "Because you're gonna go places and they know it." She was crying, but she couldn't wipe the smile off her face. We had been shunned—a mixed blessing, to be sure: to my mother it meant winning and losing everything at the same time.

Bedtime Stories

"NEVER FALL IN LOVE WITH A BLOND," MY MOTHER WARNED ME.

"Why not?" I said, though there was no point in asking. Kathi was high and in the mood for a soliloquy. She had a trove of stories that she loved to tell over and over. My role was to shut up and listen, even if I already knew where the story was headed. Most of the time, I did.

Kathi had somehow gotten wise to a scientific study that found that the human eye registers light colors before it does dark, ergo blond hair before black or brown. "Why do you think Cinderella and the Virgin Mary are always blondes? It's utter bullshit," she said. Blond hair, she went on to explain, is the first thing you see when you enter a crowded high-school gymnasium or a party in the dark woods.

"And you think it's love at first sight. But it's not. Just your eyes playing tricks," she said bitterly. "Blonds. They're the vainest people on earth."

She was obviously talking about my father.

MY PARENTS MET AS teenagers, when both of them were still high on the most dangerous intoxicant, the promise that good looks were enough to deliver them to their dreams. As the legend goes, seventeen-year-old Kathi was babysitting for a rich family that also employed a blond-haired, blue-eyed boy to mow their lawn. She watched him through the window for a few weeks before making her move.

"When are you going to take me out to dinner?"

"Tonight?" Zeke offered. He was nineteen, cute, and defenseless.

I can imagine my young mother pulling my father's blond hair, clawing his back with her long, sharp nails, my father grunting and roaring on top of her. A sickening thought for most people, it gives me great comfort now. Once there was love, brutal physical love, the kind that makes people scream, then wake up in each other's arms hungry, tired, and a little sore.

"He looked just like Robert Redford," Mum used to say.

Looking at the pictures now, I think, "Not quite . . . ," though Zeke was definitely handsome in a small-town way. My father never spoke about my mother's former beauty. He didn't need to. She bragged enough for herself. Neither of my parents tired of telling me how gorgeous everyone thought they were when they were young. Pride like this is both tyrannical and tragic, for the chief function of pride is to usher in the fall.

My parents had sufficient raw materials to achieve a level of fame in a small town, but not much more than that. Zeke was the middle child of five black-haired, brown-eyed, hockey-playing brothers, the dazzling expression of a recessive gene with his long curly blond hair, his round blue eyes, and the winning smile of a natural-born athlete. Too short even to consider going pro, he would have liked to become a hockey coach on the high-school or maybe college level. Teenage Kathi wanted to be an actress. If she had gone to college, I think my mother would soon have discovered that the stage was a better outlet for her than film. She had the kind of talents that were best seen live. She loved a monologue, and her lungs were astonishing. Although fascinating as a performance artist, Mum would have been incapable of the subtlety even bad movies have required of actors since the pictures went talkie. But I believe she could have made a name for herself in local theater, and that my father could have been a popular coach

and PE teacher if their ambitions had not already begun to wane before an unexpected pregnancy extinguished these small dreams.

NO ONE IN THE world would ever describe me as plain. I take a lot of
pride in that.

In the wrong light—fluorescent, especially—I look like a monster
in a Halloween mask, all cavernous eye socket and bulging prefrontal
lobe. But in a better light, with my head tilted just so and my lips
parted in a wry, hard-to-fake smile, my face can take on a villainous
beauty, like Cruella De Vil or Snow White's stepmother in her better
years. People often compliment my teeth. ("No braces? Ever?") I
have good hair days and bad, like anyone else. Makeup helps, but
only so much, because I have never, not for one second, been the kind
of woman who could get by on her looks alone.

My father assures me that this is a blessing. On a trip to the beach
not too long ago, the old man was moved to appraise all the aesthetic
flaws of my younger sister, his daughter by another woman, and me.
Not one to take things lying down, my sister fired back at our father
with a litany of the bad genes he'd passed down to us.

"Flat feet, oily skin, a friggin' unibrow . . ."

Zeke tried to defend himself. "You know, your mothers had some
part in it, too."

I pointed out that my sister and I spend more time, money, and
effort on hair removal than most drag queens, and that neither of
our mothers possesses this trait.

"Listen, you two girls have no idea what it's like to be really
good-looking," my father said. "It's not what you think. People are
always looking at you. They expect things from you. It's an awful lot
to live up to. And, frankly, I don't think either of you could have
handled it." He smiled to himself and ran his fingers through his hair.

"Whatcha doing, Dad?" my sister railed. "Counting how many
strands are still left?"

"I'd feel sorry for your future husbands," my father said, grinning, "but who would ever be crazy enough to marry cows like you?"

"It's a miracle we don't have fatal eating disorders," I told him, the perfect riposte, laced with guilt and the threat of debilitating illness. It must have had an impact, because the old man felt bad enough to offer a concession.

"You were pretty cute when you were little."

Isn't every mammal? We're all ridiculously cute before we move on to solid foods. It's a trick of evolution. Who would put up with us otherwise? As the darling glow of infancy wore off, the concomitants of maturity—my real face, my real character—began to emerge, and I couldn't help noticing the puzzled expressions I'd begun to elicit from adults. I hit a particularly awkward phase when I was seven, peaking in ugliness around fifth grade. By junior high, my mother could stand it no more.

"I'm not leaving this house with you until you put on some friggin' makeup and do something to that rat's nest you call hair."

I had no idea what she was talking about. As far back as I can remember, I had trained my eyes to avoid reflective surfaces. On a good day, I was and still am often startled by what the mirror has to offer. I don't know who it is staring back, but it's not—that *can't* be—me. On a bad day, this disorientation can get gothic. I will start to imagine that one of my eyes is bigger than the other. If I stare too long, it begins to grow as the other eye shrinks, until I look like a helpless grotesque from Picasso's *Guernica*. I have a talent for turning an invisibly clogged pore into a gaping wound, and, like most women in the industrialized world, I sometimes hallucinate that my legs are as thick as sequoias.

During my late childhood, I hid inside Double XL sweatshirts. I was in junior high when the nineties grunge-rock movement arrived. Though I was never cool enough to commit to the whole punk-rock aesthetic, I finally had both an explanation and an excuse for my billowing sweaters. I learned too late that it actually takes a lot of effort to look rebellious and morose, and my nihilism, however authentic, was just plain dumpy.

My mother was a product of the seventies. If you didn't have to lie down horizontally and hold your breath to zip your fly, she felt, your pants were obviously too big. All the flannel I was buying in my early teens had her deeply concerned. One Saturday after a very satisfying afternoon of moping in my bedroom, I walked into the kitchen to pour a bowl of cereal. My mother was sitting at the kitchen table. A cigarette dangled from her wrinkled lips. She looked me up and down, the ember of her Newport bobbing in sync with the scan of her eyes. She reached out and tugged on the enormous plaid shirt I was wearing.

"Honey," she asked in a plaintive voice, "why do you always look like a fat forty-year-old lesbian?"

Around this time my mother got a job as a manicurist in a full-service beauty salon, and her co-workers persuaded me to bob my long, tangled hair. It was a ruse, I soon learned. Once they got me in their clutches these women held me down on a chair in the back room of the salon, swabbed my upper lip and eyebrows with hot wax, then ripped it off.

"Jesus Christ!" I screamed.

"You have to suffer for beauty," they cackled. There was a gaggle of them, all small-town beauticians with electric tans and darkly penciled lips that made them look as if they were wearing masks. The smell of coffee and cigarettes wafted from their mouths as they hovered uncomfortably close and, one by one, plucked the more stubborn hairs from my face.

I have come to understand this moment in my life as a humanitarian act. Twelve-year-old girls aren't supposed to have mustaches, and mine had been there since I was eight. For the sake of dignity, it had to go. While I didn't twirl around my bedroom singing "I Feel Pretty" after the women in my mother's salon worked their sadistic magic, I could look at a mirror without imagining that a lesser primate was looking back in the reflection. And who knew what puberty would bring? Maybe one day I *would* become beautiful.

Shortly after the makeover, while I was organizing one of the many heaps of clutter that Mum loved to amass in our tiny home, I stumbled upon a picture that crushed my hope of ever becoming an object of beauty. It was a black-and-white photo of twenty-year-old

Kathi standing in the glassy stream of a waterfall, naked except for a microscopic bikini bottom. Her arms are folded over her small but perfect breasts, her head is tilted back, and there's a smile on her face that suggests a night of marathon sex.

"Mum, who took this picture?"

"My God," she gasped. "Your father." She snatched the photo from me and considered it. "You're in there, too, Nikki."

Hidden beneath the taut skin of her stomach, I am something bigger than bacteria but smaller than a tadpole, a whorling system of cells that my mother's antibodies still recognize as an invasion. It was the first visual proof I'd ever found of one of my mother's favorite bedtime stories: "How My Only Child Came into the World." A trashy, extravagant creation myth, I heard it as often as other kids heard "The Three Little Pigs."

MY PARENTS SPENT JANUARY of 1979 in Hawaii. Like many New Englanders, they'd saved their money all year so that they could get away for the coldest, darkest month of the winter. My mother discovered that she was pregnant a few weeks into their trip. According to my father, this was a performance she reenacted every month. (Whether I came into the world by pure accident or by womankind's oldest trick is still a matter of debate.) After he realized that my mother's story was actually true, my father packed his bags and hopped on the next plane back to Boston. I don't think I've met a man who wouldn't do the same thing. He was twenty-two years old and just as terrified as she was. My mother stayed in their youth hostel and told everyone her story of abandonment, full of tears and theatrical gestures, riding on her beauty enough for strangers to buy her food and drive her around the island. She met a native Pacific Islander with mahogany skin and a giant belly, who offered to save her reputation by marrying her. This was Mum's favorite part of the story.

". . . so this big Samoan says to me, 'Let me give your baby a name.' 'Fuck you,' I tell him. 'I'm giving this baby *my* name.' " In her next breath she added, "He wasn't the only one, you know. I was beautiful, and skinnier than you are now. *Everyone* wanted to marry me."

As the son of devout Catholics, Zeke also asked my mother to marry him when she finally returned to Massachusetts, but she refused him in similar fashion. For the following months she claims to have gone completely sober, the first of only two sober spells in her adult life. She turned twenty-one that summer and in the fall I was born. She didn't go back on her promise and gave me her last name.

This is not to say that she didn't seriously consider all her options first. When I was in fifth grade, my mother confessed that she had made an appointment to abort me. Her brother drove her to the clinic, but she refused to go in. She could have made this decision at home and saved him the trip. It was the seventies. There was an energy crisis, gas prices through the roof. But that would not have been a fitting scene for the turning point in her drama.

"I was crying and crying, Nikki. My brother kept saying, 'Go in there. Don't be stupid!' But I couldn't do it. I just couldn't get out of the car."

Later in the pregnancy, my mother also told me, she had set in motion a possible adoption, contacting an agency and filling out forms for prospective parents. Somewhere in the world my long-lost adoptive parents sat in a lonely house waiting for me to arrive. I spent countless hours imagining them, rewriting the script of *Annie,* so that instead of a redhead in an orphanage it starred a mangy brunette removed from her home by Social Services.

Betcha they're smart! Betcha they're cool!
Vegetarian lunch box at my Waldorf school!
The story of how I actually learned about my almost-adoption is less a Broadway musical than something out of a daytime soap opera.

In seventh grade I was invited to a summer pool party. Kids from other schools would be there, including boys. When my mother heard this, she demanded that I wear a bikini, a hot-pink one that she picked out herself. "Please, Honey! Wear it for me," she begged. I covered it up with a T-shirt that came down to my knees. This is how I gleaned my first lesson in attracting the attention of boys and men—that desire is only intensified by concealment and withholding. When my wet T-shirt stuck like a second skin with a neon bathing suit peeking through, I found myself in the middle of a swarm of boys, all of them constantly readjusting their shorts. The cutest one, I thought, was a boy from Salem named Seamus. I mentioned this to a girl at the party and a commitment ceremony soon followed. That's all it takes in seventh grade—vague interest and a series of emissaries to handle the details.

The next day Seamus and I had our first conversation on the phone. We had little in common apart from the fact that we shared the same birthday and were both die-hard fans of U2. I'd prepared for our chat by writing down a list of things to talk about. Item one was which song from *The Joshua Tree* best represented our love.

"Um, I don't know," Seamus said.

Fine. I moved on to the topic of our cosmically aligned birthdays. "Where were you born?" I asked him.

"Beverly Hospital," he said.

"So was I! That means we were there together as babies!"

I was in raptures. How could any girl be lucky enough to meet her soul mate in junior high? I would wait until I was eighteen to move in with him, twenty-one to have our first child, just like my mother, only the situation would be slightly more dignified by a legal marriage.

Kathi overheard me talking to Seamus and she came running into my bedroom. "Tell him to put his mother on," she said, and took the phone from me. The two women spoke for a while, my mother's voice hushed and excited. Afterward, Mum sat on my bed and told me her version of my first days in the world outside her body:

Seamus and I both had young single mothers planning to give their babies up for adoption. The hospital put these two girls in the same room, thinking it would spare them the pain of sharing a room with happy families who had conceived their babies on purpose. Or, as my mother liked to explain, "They wanted to consolidate the two whores in the *Scarlet Letter* room." Seamus's mother actually went through with the adoption, while my mother had again changed her mind.

"It was a whim," she admitted. "You were so small and hairy and you looked vaguely Chinese. I couldn't get over your feet."

And so my mother had met my seventh-grade boyfriend long before I did, and had shared intimate postpartum words with the birth mother he had never known.

Mum loved to relive moments like these. Stories of her lost youth were our nightly bedtime ritual. She never read books to me. She wanted to, but whenever she tried to read she said the letters jumped around and flipped backward on the page. It was frustrating, and also humiliating. "Mummy's not smart," she'd say, pouting. Stupidity was the diagnosis that her teachers in the Danvers public schools had given her. *Stunata* was the word in her mother's native tongue. Dyslexia was not even mentioned until late in my mother's senior year of high school. By then Kathi had carved her own path that was more successful.

"I was beautiful and popular," she told me. "Everyone worshipped me. And you know what? I was nice to everyone. Even the geeks. The geeks *loved* me. I won class president four years in a row by a landslide. The geek vote was crucial. My senior year, no one even bothered to run against me."

The crowning achievement of her presidency, she told me one night as she sat smoking at the foot of my bed, was a screening of the 1930s cult film *Reefer Madness* in the high-school auditorium. A natural-born entrepreneur, my mother saw her position in student government as an opportunity to make some money for herself. She and a friend went in on an ounce of grass, rolled dozens of joints with a little tobacco sprinkled in them to make the marijuana stretch, and sold them at the movie screening on the sly.

"We made more money from the first showing than the PTA had collected all friggin' year!" she said. "It was a coup, Nikki! Your mother was something."

Her voice always became kittenish when she told these stories. Her eyelashes would flutter as though she were flirting with me.

There were fables about rich boyfriends she refused to marry because she was too in love with my father (though not so deliriously in love that she remained faithful when a rich guy asked her out). She told me about the night three different dates showed up at the house, and my grandmother had to send each one away because Kathi had stood them all up for a fourth guy she'd met at the gas station. With the same strung-out lyricism, she would recall in graphic detail the afternoon she was raped by a cousin, and then again by a boy in ninth grade. There was the fairy tale of her first acid trip, when she was eleven years old and her older brother's friend slipped a tab of LSD into her soda can. She was at a slumber party when the phantasmagoria began.

"I don't think I've been so scared in my life, Nikki. I thought bats were flying out of my friend's wallpaper and getting caught in my hair."

"Tell me a story about *me*," I'd beg her. "About when I was a baby."

"Did I tell you about the time when you were brand-new, lying on Nonna's bed, reaching for me, and you were so cute I wanted to hit you? I mean really hit you! I leaned over and bit your foot and you started to cry. Oh, the face you made! Sometimes I would bite you just so you would make that face again. It was so fuckin' cute! Do you remember the time I pulled over on the side of the highway and contemplated leaving you there?"

Yes. Vividly. But I let her tell it again. I never interrupted my mother's reveries. They were too important to her. She so badly wanted an audience, and I just wanted her to be near me, to smell the acrid mint of her cigarettes, feel the weight of her body pressing down my blanket. Our little nighttime chats. Was she trying to scare me? To push me away? It had the opposite effect. I clung even tighter. There's a natural phase most girls go through, spurred on by hormonal upsurges and awakenings of consciousness, when they abruptly begin to despise their mother. Not me. The older I got, the more terrified I was of losing her violent, temperamental love.

Sometimes Kathi would sit on my bed and tell me that she was dying. She had cancer, possibly AIDS, and that was why she needed to take so many pills. I would cry myself to sleep, her looming death a kind of apocalypse I dreaded night after aching night. Until years later, when I started hoping for it.

But I'm getting ahead of myself.

"Mumma, tell me a *good* story," I would say, before all that happened.

"Did I tell you about the time Rose Kennedy smiled at me when I was almost nine months pregnant with you?"

"Who's Rose Kennedy?"

"She was the president's mother and she knew a good thing when she saw it."

"Tell me more," I said, rubbing the cuff of her sleeve between my fingers.

"When you came out and they showed you to me, my first words were 'Oh, no! She has her father's dented chin!' But you were so smart. It was obvious even before you could talk. I remember one day looking at you in your car seat—a shaft of light was coming in through the window and you wanted to hold it. You kept reaching for it and making little baby fists with your hands. You were trying to hold on to the light. And I said to my mother, 'This kid is going to be brilliant.' "

The Ring That Got Stuck on My Finger

DANVERS, MASSACHUSETTS, THE TOWN I GREW UP IN, WAS ONCE infamous in the annals of American history, though most people have never heard of it. In 1692, the Puritans of Danvers (then called Salem Village) sent nineteen of their citizens to the gallows for practicing witchcraft. The actual hanging of these witches took place in Salem proper, and it was this neighboring city that went down in popular history. The city of Salem has a witch museum where, for eight bucks, teenage drama students in heavy eyeliner escort tourists through a series of dioramas. Mannequins who once modeled leisurewear at Sears now find themselves posed in the mischief of that pitiless New England winter. Red lights strobe below them, and hidden speakers blare the staticky screams of a black Sabbath.

Up the street from the Witch Museum, the history of collective hysteria and Calvinist dissent has been immortalized with a bronze statue of Elizabeth Montgomery, from TV's *Bewitched*. There she sits sidesaddle on her broomstick, smiling vacuously at the surrounding red-brick streets. This part of Salem is lined with souvenir shops where you can buy T-shirts and tote bags stamped with the generic outline of a witch, as well as peanut brittle, tarot cards, whoopee cushions, and bongs.

In Danvers there are no gift shops. Only a few houses remain from those dark last days of the seventeenth century. One of them belonged to Rebecca Nurse, the oldest victim of the witch trials, and it is open to the public free of charge. The site is half a mile from my father's house. We had to drive by it every time we went to the mall. I would always crane my neck to watch the house whiz past the window, my heart pumping as I looked down the dirt road and imagined what it would feel like to be hanged.

BOTH OF MY PARENTS were born and raised in Danvers, a place they have only ever left for a couple of weeks on vacation. It's a small town breathing life into a slowly dying phenomenon: a place where everyone knows everybody else. Members of my family can't drive to the post office without beeping or getting beeped at by friends of theirs. For me, Danvers exists as a collection of businesses—sub shops, roast-beef shops, pizza joints, and nail salons. I spent the first half of my life in this town and collected not one friend in the Zip Code. My father tried to integrate me every spring by signing me up for girls' softball, and every spring I backed out. Asthma was my excuse, social terror and poor coordination my reasons. My neighborhood was teeming with boys and girls my age, but I didn't play with them. They were morons, and I had a TV set up with premium cable in my bedroom.

But that is a bitter revisionist's history. The truth is, the kids on Eden Glen Avenue had rejected me long before I had a chance to disdain them. At one point or another, every woman on the street had had her turn babysitting me. The children at these neighbors' houses regarded me like a strange vegetable their mothers had brought home from the grocery store, something they probably wouldn't like but could tolerate for dinner once in a while. I'd watch these kids dump their book bags after school, then run outside to do whatever it was they did in their sunny, shrieking groups. I never ran after them. It didn't occur to me that I should. Instead, I would sit at their kitchen tables and quietly do my homework. When I was finished I would get started on the next night's homework, and the next, teaching myself a whole unit of arithmetic or geography while I waited for my mother to come home.

When I heard Mum's car choking in the driveway, I would run to her as fast as I could, without thanking my babysitter, without even saying goodbye. One day as we pulled out, a gang of kids was chasing one another in what I guess was a game of tag. They stopped and moved to the side of the street to allow my mother's car to pass. The kids glared at me through the window. I glared back.

"Why don't you ask them if you can play," my mother suggested.

"Why?" I asked. Mum shrugged and let it go.

Sometimes, when she wanted to torture me, Kathi would go behind my back and invite the neighbors' kids, Lisa and Donald, to come over and play with me. This was her way of punishing me for saying something affectionate about someone other than her. I couldn't stand Lisa and Donald, and she knew it. They were pale and meek in a way that would have ended their lives early if it weren't for the invention of antibiotics. Someone, maybe my mother, had gotten the mistaken idea that these kids and I had sickliness in common, except that I usually exaggerated my symptoms to get attention, whereas Donald's and Lisa's scoliosis was quite real.

My mother would wait until I was engrossed in a movie, then she would sneak up the street to collect the sniveling agents of her revenge. I would hear a knock on my bedroom door, and there would be Mum, ushering Lisa and Donald inside. They were such sad, wooden little kids, with mouse-brown hair and wet, gray eyes the color of sidewalk puddles on a murky day. Like me, they weren't too successful making friends with the other kids on Eden Glen Avenue, although they were both crazy and brave enough to continue trying.

What was I supposed to do with them?

"*Crimes and Misdemeanors* is on. You missed the first half hour." I'd seen it before and was willing to catch them up, but only if they asked. I offered them a seat on my bed, which neither accepted. They just stood there blinking at me.

"What would you do if someone on the school bus offered you drugs?" Donald asked me gravely.

I knew from previous playdate punishments that he and Lisa had learned everything they needed to know about life from the network after-school specials that were so popular in the 1980s. It took all my strength not to smack him.

"I think our father's an . . . an . . . alcoholic," Lisa confessed on another visit. She looked at Donald, who was wringing his hands. Tears welled up on the pink rims of their eyes. I was not moved. Even when these kids were happy, their voices quavered as though on the verge of tears.

"So what?" I said.

I swear—I didn't mean to hurt their feelings. I just wanted them to go away so I could finish my movie. Gluttons for punishment (their father probably *was* an alcoholic), they would come back again and again. Every time Donald got a new computer game or Lisa got a tube of lip gloss, they would run over to my house, thinking, for some reason, that this concerned me.

"What do they want?" I would yell from my bedroom when I heard knocking at our door. As my mother had the kind of guests who just let themselves in, we both knew these visitors were for me.

"They probably want to play with you," my mother would yell back.

Neither of us would bother to get up from our respective beds to answer the door. I'd turn up the volume of my television.

"Tell them I'm sick."

"You tell them."

"Please! I called in sick for *you* last week."

Even if I had nurtured solid friendships with the neighborhood kids, nothing could have redeemed me after the summer I got head lice. My mother made me walk up and down the street and confess this to any neighbor whose house I'd ever entered. Like a registered sex offender, I had to knock on their doors and identify myself as the carrier of a plague.

"You should probably throw away all your hairbrushes," I said, scratching behind my ears. "Wash your pillowcases and towels in hot water. It wouldn't hurt to dump in some bleach."

One group of girls saved a hairbrush that I may or may not have touched and sealed it in a Ziploc bag. "The Nikki brush," they called it. It became a weapon whose power mushroomed with every succeeding year. They would throw it at one another and scream, the way young girls do, with churlish delight. Even Lisa had been party to this. Poor thing, she was probably grateful that, for once, the joke was not on her.

THANK GOD I DIDN'T go to school with those kids. It was one of my mother's few life goals that I never set foot in the Danvers public schools. She had endured twelve years in that system, and what good had it done her? Within a week of my sixth birthday, she enrolled me at the local Catholic school, St. Mary of the Annunciation, then helped someone move a brick of cocaine and paid the full year's tuition, twelve hundred dollars, in cash.

I would have to wear a uniform every day, which I loved. From a distance, I would appear just like everyone else. "It's hideous," my mother said. She rubbed the fabric between her fingers. "Ugh. Polyester." She looked ready to spit.

The jumper was red-and-green plaid. Underneath we had to wear a white button-down blouse with the compulsory rounded collar. *Never* pointed collars, I found out the hard way. Pointed collars, I guess, were for Protestants, Jews, and tramps. Only a sedate shade of red or hunter-green socks was allowed, and our sweaters were supposed to match our socks as closely as possible. The school sent home notices to reinforce the dress code, and I seemed to get these notices more often than the other kids. It needled my mother's vain heart to see her only child disappear in a crowd, so she would outfit me in sparkly teal stockings and cherry-red patent-leather shoes, marking me as someone different. Hers.

I wore my uniform every day that first year. I wore it on weekends. I wore it to bed. I wore it so much that the hem of the skirt unraveled. For some reason, I decided that the person who should fix this for me was the school nurse. I remember the way she took a long look at me, brushed my knotted hair, and cleaned my ears with a Q-tip. "You silly girl," she said, laughing. "Just tell your mother to sew the hem."

Asking my mother for help could be risky. It required perfect timing. Her waking hours were mapped by a wave of chemical highs and lows. If I asked her to hem my skirt, I could get a cold shrug of the shoulders. I could get a temper tantrum and an ashtray flung very close to but not exactly at my head. I could get a wild shopping spree for a new wardrobe but not a new uniform. I could get roller skates, a puppy, or the following: "Get the fuck away from me. I can't stand the sound of you breathing right now." I could get kicked out of my own house, banished to my grandmother's, or simply ignored for the next three days.

I stayed up late one night, listening to my mother and her friends talking and laughing outside my bedroom window. People were coming in and out of the house to blow coke off the kitchen table. I knew when it was my mother and not someone else entering our apartment by the sound the screen door made when it slid open and shut. Like an animal, I could sense my mother's body from far away.

Her feet pounded down the hall toward my room. Despite Mum's diet of cigarettes and cocaine, she was about thirty pounds overweight at this point, and growing fatter by the day. She burst through my door and collapsed onto my bed as if she had just had a massive heart attack and died. I waited for a moment, holding my breath, smiling so wide my cheeks hurt.

Please don't die. Please don't be mad at me. Please.

She lifted her head and looked at me. Her long bangs fell into her face and I couldn't see her eyes. Then she smiled. That big, screeching laugh. Okay, I exhaled. We're okay.

"Mum, my uniform is ripped." I showed her the falling hem.

"Oh, shit," she said. She sat up and pulled the chain on my bedside lamp. Her pupils were almost gone, small and black as flakes of pepper. She removed a long thread from the skirt and squinted at it in the light.

"I have an idea!" she snapped. She ran out of the room and came back with scissors and a roll of duct tape. She cut out strips to fit the length of the pleats and, voilà, my uniform was hemmed.

"You are a *genius!*" I hugged her neck.

"I do my best," she agreed.

Her work was flawless, until the hot spring day when the glue began to melt and again my hem fell at recess, this time rimmed with gooey silver tape.

MY FIRST-GRADE TEACHER WAS Sister Agnes, a short, stern woman who had given up a large family fortune to become a nun. She wore pastel blouses and nylon skirts and beige sneakers whose soles had worn down over the years to a smooth, eerily silent rubber pad that allowed her to sneak up on her students unawares. Even on the coldest winter days, I could track the brown elastic of Sister Agnes's knee-highs as they slowly descended her thick, veiny calves. On either side of the chalkboard, Sister Agnes had stapled a picture of equal size at equal height, both bordered with a scalloped frame of green construction paper. On the right was the Virgin Mary holding the Baby Jesus on her lap. Jesus sat with absurdly dignified posture for an infant, a gold disk like a plate perfectly balanced on his head. Mary was a luminous blonde with dark, hooded eyes that looked exhausted and a little bit stoned. On the left side of the chalkboard was a signed photograph of Larry Bird. Sister Agnes was an old Irish-Catholic New Englander who, during basketball season, would include the Boston Celtics in our morning petitions. To this day, whenever Larry Bird's name is mentioned, I feel moved to bow my head and pray.

One morning at school I was sharpening my pencil when I noticed that my finger had become swollen and discolored. The night before, I'd bought a twenty-five-cent ring from a toy dispenser at the grocery store. The ring was painted gold, with a ruby rhinestone sparkling at the center. I couldn't wait to flaunt it to all the kids at school. I fell asleep wearing it, having tried and failed to pry it off before going to bed. Now the circulation had been restricted for hours and my finger was turning blue. I showed it to Sister Agnes, who tried to pull the ring off while I stood beside her desk, then took me into the girls' bathroom and lathered my hand with soap. When that didn't work, Sister told me to keep scrubbing while she went to the cafeteria. She returned with a jug of corn oil to grease my finger. She pulled. I pulled. The ring would not budge.

So far that year, I'd been sent home from school for having bronchitis, strep throat, and a condition that can only be described as hysterical vomiting. There were days I arrived crying so hard I had to be sent to the nurse's office, where I would lie on a cot until lunchtime. I was late as often as I was on time, and sometimes I took weeks off from school with neither a medical excuse nor a decent lie to explain my absence. One day I showed up wearing no underwear beneath my uniform. My whole body ignites with shame when I remember the morning I sat cross-legged in our circle for story time, and Sister Agnes hopped up and yanked me into another room where I sat alone until a clean pair of underpants could be procured for me to wear.

"Call your mother," Sister Agnes told me now as we stood in the dark, tiled lavatory. Her hands clamped angrily around my shoulders, and I could feel her body quaking.

By that time Mum didn't have a car anymore. The Shitbox had met its inexorable end and we now relied on friends, family, and strangers for rides. From the front office I saw a black-and-yellow taxicab pull up to the school and my mother step out. It was a warm spring day. The trees were decorated with fuzzy green buds, and pale tulips had begun poking through the mud. My mother flirted shamelessly with the cabdriver during the ride to the hospital. His name was Michael, and he said that he had graduated from high school with my mother. "I played trumpet in the marching band," he told her. "I had thick glasses."

"I didn't remember him at all," my mother said to me later. "Of course, he knew exactly who *I* was."

Now Kathi was a single mother who needed a ride and Michael

was the man who picked her up. We waited in the hospital for nearly three hours before a doctor saw me. I showed him my finger proudly, swollen and blue in its little vise. The doctor cut the ring off with an electric saw the size of a dime. When we left the hospital, Michael was still waiting for us. And this was the man my mother eventually married.

Echo

FOR TWO YEARS IN MY LATE TWENTIES I WORKED A RELIEF SHIFT at the National Domestic Violence Hotline. We fielded calls from all over the country, around three thousand a day, hundreds more if our number was mentioned on that afternoon's episode of *Oprah*. For eight hours straight I'd listen to the living nightmares of strangers, stories so hateful they made the average horror flick look tender. A lot of them I wish I could forget. One caller told me about the morning that her husband beckoned her to walk with him into the remote edges of his ranch. Pointing with his finger, he indicated how far and wide his land stretched; then, in the stillness of the morning, he explained to his wife exactly how he was going to kill her—what method and tools he would use to dispose of her body—if she ever tried to leave him. I talked to another woman who had to change both her and her daughter's names and Social Security numbers, effectively erasing their identities, because her ex-boyfriend, a cop, had stalked them all the way across the country. There were women who were forbidden to switch on a lightbulb while their lovers were out of the house, and mail-order brides who had been raped so severely that they required reconstructive surgery just to take a pee. One woman called simply to say, "The police won't help me. I have to tell *someone*—if I'm found dead tomorrow, I want you to know this man's name."

I kept these women on the line as long as I could, afraid of what might happen to them when they hung up. I got repeat callers who knew me by name, and for whom I would beg the local shelters to find a bed. At home I would fold my hands against my heart and ask Someone, Anyone, to protect these hunted women scattered across the country, then throw in a quick, half-superstitious Hail Mary for good measure.

If only all battered wives could be so conveniently sympathetic. The monoliths of abuser and abused cast stark shadows across the American conscience, when the real picture is something more complicated, a prism that captures the full spectrum of good and evil and shatters it into fractured pieces of color and light. I spoke to several women who balked at the idea of state-subsidized housing; they informed me that they would rather be called "fat bitch" on a daily basis by their boyfriends than downgrade in apartment square footage. A sense of racist entitlement prevented many women from seeking shelter in a domestic-violence safe house. "I don't want to share a bathroom with some Hispanic lady and her ten kids," I heard more than once. "Can't your organization just give me some money so I can stay in a motel for a couple months?"

Some callers had an obstinate love of material comfort that made me want to slap them myself. These women were not slaves to their lovers or even to a violent, twisted concept of love. Their bondage was to a man's steady paycheck and the meaningless *things* it bought.

I heard stories of fear and self-hatred that echoed my own. I heard a lot of broken records. Sometimes I would be so numb at the end of an eight-hour shift I'd find myself stabbing my thighs with an uncoiled paperclip while the caller on my headset described being beaten with a power cord. This particular caller didn't want to involve the police or get a restraining order or even break up with the man who did this to her. She told me she'd stolen his credit card and treated herself to a shopping spree instead. I could feel my eyeballs twitching as I listened to her, and buried somewhere inside my chest the beating of a cold, mad heart.

———

I WAS FOUR YEARS old when my father married his girlfriend, Carla. My mother was forbidden to attend the wedding. It was a slight she never forgot.

"They made this big deal, telling everyone in Danvers not to tell me where the ceremony was," she told me. "Like I was going to burst in and stop the show." My mother rolled her eyes. "*Please*. I just wanted to see you in your little flower-girl dress."

Kathi had known Carla in high school. In the shallowest sense, they were women of the same ilk—short, Italian-American brunettes. Girls like this can sniff each other out from across the room at a party, and either become best friends or instantly, rabidly despise each other.

"Carla thinks she's won some big prize," my mother said when she heard about my father's engagement. "Ha! She's getting exactly what she deserves."

And yet when my father was in one of his moods, clearing the kitchen table of dishes with one impulsive sweep of his arm, punching holes into the walls, swinging a baseball bat inside the house, it was my mother's kitchen where Carla went to recoup. A couple of times a year, my stepmother would appear at the front door in tears.

"Oh, Jesus, Carla," my mother would say. "Sit down. Relax."

"Kathi, you know how he gets."

"Believe me. I remember."

For some sick reason, Carla's crises brought out my mother's perky side. Kathi would practically chirp as she whipped up something for Carla to eat. My mother and stepmother would sit at the kitchen table smoking cigarettes and snacking like two girlfriends on their lunch break. When Carla decided that she was ready to go back home, my mother respectfully showed her the door.

"She's not the brightest person in the world," Kathi said of Carla. "And she's lazy, always has been. The woman has two speeds—slow and stop. But, Christ, if I had to live with your father, I'd want to sleep all day, too."

MY STEPMOTHER WAS THE youngest of three girls, the only member
of her immediate family who was born in America. Her parents and
sisters moved from Italy after World War II ended. Carla's mother,
Elda, was a big, square-faced woman with a loud, brusque voice,
who in her sixty-one years as an American citizen never learned to
speak English. She didn't need to. If Elda wanted something, she
would simply holler and thrash while everyone around her scram-
bled to figure out what had to be done.

My father hated Elda so much that he refused to go to his
mother-in-law's house even on Christmas Day. The one time I remember Elda visiting our house, she commandeered my father's yard
tools and did some pruning on the birch Dad loved more than any
other tree in the yard.

"Get away from that," Zeke yelled when he saw what she was
doing. Elda snapped back at him in Italian, a long, Fascist-sounding
rant, then went home. A few months later, the birch tree died.

"She killed it," my father said. "She did it on purpose."

My stepmother grew up to be the exact opposite of her mother: a
quiet, sluggish woman with her head in the clouds. Carla's only expressed ambition in life was to become a flight attendant or a florist.
She's been a waitress and a hospital tech, sometimes simultaneously,
for the almost thirty years that I've known her. A devoted mother,
she always made sure that her work schedule allowed her to go to my
brother's and sister's hockey games. She has probably spent half her
adult life shivering in ice rinks, cheering for her offspring as they
skated in circles and clobbered other kids with their sticks.

As soon as he married Carla, my father bought back his childhood home from the couple who had bought it from his widowed
mother. It's a New England cape with weather-beaten shingles that
look like slices of burned toast. The house is small, but the backyard
is one of the biggest on the street, with room enough for a garden
and a decent game of Wiffle ball. At the edge of the yard is a hill that
my father gutted of trees and terraced with long wooden planks he

scavenged from the town dump. Below the hill is a meadow of wild-flowers and reeds. Every winter the Danvers Fire Department floods the meadow with water so that it can freeze into a public skating park. Zeke taught my brother, sister, and me how to skate there by pushing a plastic milk crate around the ice until we were sturdy enough to glide away on our own. He and his four brothers all learned to skate the same way, in the same meadow, a generation before us.

I spent Sundays, Mondays, and Tuesdays at my father's when—if—visitations were being properly observed, and I cannot recall a single day in my life when his house was not under construction. Zeke has remodeled the interior himself slowly over the years, tear-ing apart floors and knocking down walls. He works room by room, often leaving a project unfinished for several months in the spring only to resume it later in the winter. There have been spells when we washed our dishes in the bathtub, or shared one toilet among six people. Inevitably, in the rubble of these renovations, my father will find something—a baseball card, a bag of marbles—that whispers to him from a lifetime before us. At one point, my father's mother moved back into the house for the penultimate stage of her Alzheim-er's, and the former matriarch now wandered the half-renovated rooms like a quiet, baffled toddler. Here was the same backyard and the birch tree that my father and his father planted together. Here were the slate front steps, the blackened shingles, the meadow. Here we were, life circling around once more.

ONE DAY, AS I was lying in my father's backyard, I pulled a four-leaf clover out of the ground. I was stunned. I hadn't been looking for a four-leaf clover—or anything else, for that matter. It just seemed to find my fingers as they absently stroked the thick, glossy lawn. When I realized what it was, I ran to show Zeke, who was up on a ladder de-nuding his blighted birch. At first he didn't believe me and continued stripping branches. I was nearly five years old, wont to see the world as a magical place. I hounded him until he finally stopped to look.

"Well, for crying out loud," he said, taking the clover in his hand. "You really did."

We went inside to show my stepmother, who was standing at the cluttered kitchen counter. She was always overwhelmed by something—groceries to put away, dishes to wash, dinner to cook.

"Isn't that nice," she said without looking.

I placed the four-leaf clover on a scrap of paper, which my father dated, and we sealed it between two squares of plastic wrap. Then we had to find somewhere safe to keep it.

"We need a book," my father said.

Besides my stepmother's cookbooks, there were only two books in the house at that time, the Audubon Society's *Birds of America* and a tattered Bible crammed on a basement shelf underneath a shoebox full of loose change. My father and I both agreed that the bird book, which was big and had a hard cover, would work best. We tucked the clover among a spread of blue jays perched on flowering branches that vanished into the margins.

Zeke and I returned to the backyard. He continued chopping down his tree. I peeled swatches of moss off a stone and arranged them into the map of an imaginary world full of countries I named after girls: Victoria, Cassandra, and the Islands of Zoë.

And again without trying, I found another four-leaf clover. I ran to show my father. He wrinkled his forehead in disbelief and perhaps a tinge of envy. He'd already taken one break that afternoon. He wasn't going to interrupt his work again.

"Go ask Carla to help you," he said.

Carla was in her early thirties then, and still a very pretty woman. She and my father had recently returned from their honeymoon in Hawaii, and she was a quarter-moon pregnant with my younger brother. I went inside and found her standing before her Sisyphean mountain of housework. When I showed her the four-leaf clover this time, she twisted around and glared at me. Spite crackled in the air between us.

"Another one?" she cried.

———

CARLA INTRODUCES HERSELF TO my friends as "the Wicked Step-mother." She laughs from the belly whenever she says it. I do, too. I love everything about her self-appointed nickname. First, the use of the definite article: Carla does not see herself as *a* wicked stepmother but *the* Wicked Stepmother, a singular character of importance, even if it is an antagonist's role. Second, the allusion to a fairy tale is as funny as it is true. I have an undeniable Cinderella complex. When I get into a martyr's frenzy of vacuuming, no one is better than my Wicked Stepmother at putting me back in my place. "Nik, you're a legend in your own mind" is her chosen refrain.

But the best of all this wicked-stepmother business is: *she said it, not me.*

Because there have been moments of wickedness. Oh, yes. Vicious, primal battles, icy competitions so subtle and silent that they seemed to be fought on a molecular level, and then some scenes so transparently nasty they bordered on cliché.

Like the Fourth of July party I can't let go of. One of Carla's friends asked me what I wanted to be when I grew up. "A doctor," I told the woman. I was eight years old and it was the most interesting and noble thing I could think of becoming.

"How do you know what you're going to be?" Carla snapped. "For all you know, you'll be pregnant by the time you're sixteen."

I don't imagine it was easy for her. Three days a week she was responsible for feeding, bathing, and supervising another woman's child. That this child had the same smile as her former sexual rival was an added insult. That this child was also demanding and imperious, telling her how she ought to run her household, that she was so oversensitive she cried at the drop of a hat—I doubt any of this was ever a part of Carla's life plan. I'd arrive at her house in dirty clothes, my snarly hair clumped in Caucasian dreadlocks. My father would hand me over to his wife so that he could do whatever work there was to be done on the house. She'd shampoo me in the bathtub, then sit me in the middle of the living-room floor and drag a brush through my knotted hair. I made a point of screaming loud enough for the neighbors to hear.

"Fay Wray," she'd say with a shudder. "You're an actress, just like your mother."

From a safe distance I can see how, in Carla's cosmology, I was both a burden and a threat. Even without a precocious and needy stepdaughter to weigh her down, Carla was failing miserably to manage the things in life that were legitimately hers. The house usually looked like a disaster site, the cupboards were stuffed with junk food and empty of essentials, the checkbook was overdrawn and the credit cards had been maxed. She and my father were always in a screaming match, and my little brother was plagued by night terrors.

Three o'clock in the morning is an ugly hour. Little good ever comes to people who are awake to see it. It was at this time that my brother would be summoned from his bed as though hypnotized. He'd walk around the house sobbing in his footed pajamas, his eyes wide open but far away in a dream. No one knew what to do. Carla and Zeke had taken him to see neurologists in Boston. "Stop feeding him sugar after four P.M." was their professional advice. But Carla could never say no to her bambino, and my brother would go to sleep with a belly full of candy and soda. At night she would follow her inconsolable son from room to room, feebly trying to reason with him. "Wake up. You're having a bad dream." This would go on for about half an hour, until my father finally got up and the pageant began.

The three of them were locked inside their collective nightmare. I wandered in the dark behind them, invisible and restless as a ghost. It was as though I wasn't there. A blessing, I suppose, to be excluded from the drama. Until one night Carla shouted at my father:

"Why don't you ever hit *her*?"

Carla pointed to where I stood clutching the banister, and the feeling of a rusty shiv pierced my ribs. *Why* was not an interrogative adverb in this sentence; it was a modal of suggestion, as in, Why don't we invite the neighbors over for supper? Why don't we go apple picking this weekend? Why don't we try to be more egalitarian with our violence?

To my stepmother I was an assistant, a sometime friend, a scape-goat, and a competitor. Then, in the strangest turn of events, I became her personal hotline. When my father's anger turned violent from time to time, she didn't call my mother or her own family or friends. She called me.

"Leave him, Carla," I have told her again and again. The fact that "him" is my father is something we both seem to block out.

"Well, his TV is on top of my oak bureau and my TV is all the way in the cellar. I can't lift that thing by myself."

Furniture and fear. I've heard it all before.

ANOTHER MEMORY, ANOTHER STORY. I am six years old, and my little brother is one. My stepmother tries to make me jealous of the baby, who is blond and blue-eyed and objectively much cuter than I ever was. But I'm too in love with the little meatball to feel anything but glee when I see him. Before he came along, I used to fake stom-achaches so that I could skip weekends at Dad's and stay at home with my mother. Now I can't wait for my dad to come and get me so I can go over to his house and hold the baby.

That Sunday, I'm waiting in my mother's driveway for my father to pick me up. He pulls up in his truck, and when he gets out he won't look at me. His eyes are red as wounds.

"Get in the car," he says. Those four words—never a portent of good things to come. "I have to talk to your mother."

Every pore in my skin sparks. I'm stuck there in the driveway. Waiting for something, I have no idea what. Then I hear it—my mother screaming for me, screaming for help, screaming for *me to help her*.

I run back into the apartment and see my father on top of her, his hands wrapped around her throat as he bangs her head against the thinly carpeted concrete floor. I jump on his back and pry him away, though that hardly seems possible now. Another fictive flight of memory? I don't know. But that is how I remember it, so that's what I'm telling you here. My mother scrambles to her feet and lifts me up, holding my body in front of hers like a shield, while she and my father continue yelling. Curses, tears, and threats. My father drives away in his truck.

The next day Kathi walked me into school herself, something she had never done before, a necklace of bruises glowing on the delicate skin of her throat. She asked to speak to Sister Agnes alone in the hall. What did those two women say to each other? I wonder still.

I refused to go to my father's house after that, and my mother certainly didn't force me. What felt like a year later, though it was probably just a couple of months, I was with one of my aunts and some cousins downtown when we ran into my father and the baby. I hadn't seen either of them since the fight. My little brother seemed to have doubled in size. I couldn't believe the cool, confident way he sat on my father's hip. His downy yellow hair had grown into thick ringlets. His smile was so big it wrenched at my heart.

"Hey, long time no see!" my dad said, grinning. "Almost forgot what you looked like, Nik!"

"Long time no see! Almost forgot what you looked like!" my brother repeated. A perfect imitation of my father's smile dimpled his fat cheeks.

Sometime after that encounter, I resumed my weekend visits at Dad's. It was as if nothing had happened. What I remember most about my father from then on was his absence. A loosely refolded newspaper on the kitchen table, an empty mug of coffee in the sink. At breakfast I would sit in his chair at the table, hoping to catch the lingering warmth his body had left behind.

Zeke was off to work by five in the morning every weekday. On weekends, he allowed himself to sleep until six before he dived into some backyard project he'd created for himself. He has been a construction worker since he was a teenager, owned his own business for several years, then sold all his machinery and joined a labor union. His trade is paving—driveways, sidewalks, streets, and curbs. During the winter he plowed snow for the town. While everyone else in New England cursed the sky for dumping another six inches on the frozen ground, my father told me to pray for twelve more. Blizzards put food on the table four months out of the year. They kept us hovering just barely above bankruptcy. Carla's ability to max out multiple credit cards was startling. Every time Zeke managed to hack away her debt, another bill would surface with twice the interest rate. A winter without snow meant that we would be broke and Dad would be idle—the basic human recipe for family violence.

For the next two years, when I was seven and eight, I spent three days a week with my brother and stepmother more or less peacefully. At four o'clock my father returned home from work. There was always a slight jolt in the air when he entered the house, a charge that put us all on edge. My brother and I would follow him around like ducklings, from the basement to the living room to the kitchen and back again. Some days Zeke seemed to enjoy his little shadows. He'd take us into the backyard and toss a ball directly at our yellow plastic bat so that when we swung we couldn't miss. We ran around an imaginary baseball diamond and he would lift us up onto his shoulders, the champions of the world.

At other times he walked through the door with squinted eyes, scanning the room for something to destroy.

"What are you lying around for?" he would snap. "Why don't you ever play outside? Jesus, Nikki. Run around a little!"

Zeke's an athlete by nature, a laborer by culture, a blue-collar New Englander who believes that sunshine is a resource you have to earn the right to enjoy and that rest is only for the dead. If I simply read my book in the backyard, instead of on the couch, he'd leave me alone. In that big backyard I read about the spider who spun prophetic words into her web, about the lion who gave up his life for the sake of four bereft orphans, about the pioneer family in a covered wagon battling scarlet fever and blizzards. I read about the gods and goddesses of Greek antiquity, who were as real to me as the people in my family. It was amazing how much time could disappear while I was reading.

My stepmother got pregnant again. This time it was a girl. The baby arrived precisely at the moment when I was too old to play with dolls but secretly still wanted to. I met my sister for the first time when I was nine years old and she was a tiny cloud on an ultrasound. An obstetrician rubbed clear gel over Carla's stomach and with a wand projected an image of her insides onto a little TV. It looked like the faint cluster of stars in another galaxy, something immaterial and very far away.

I decided then and there in that office that, no matter what this creature turned into, I'd make her be my best friend whether she liked it or not. My mother and her sisters were always embroiled in a war that nobody ever won. My sister and I had a better chance of making it if we were on the same team.

According to the ultrasound, my fetal sister had tucked both of her hands behind her head, like a sunbather in repose, and would have to be delivered by Cesarean. My stepmother said that she, too, had been discovered in the womb with her arms in the same position. This was a revelation to me: people can resemble their parents not just in the shape of their eyes or the color of their hair but in the way that they occupy space in the world.

A year later, I came inside after reading in the backyard and the sudden contrast between the bright sunshine and the shady interior of the house blinded me. I walked through the kitchen in a dazzling blackness. When my eyes finally readjusted, I saw my stepmother and baby sister napping on the living-room couch. Carla lay on her back with her hands behind her head; my sister lay on her mother's stomach, sleeping in the same position, just as both of them had slept in the liquid dark of the womb. I looked at the shape of their bodies, one on top of the other, and whispered a single word:

"Echo."

It wasn't until much later that I understood what had happened that day. Inside me was someone new waiting to be born, not a baby, like my sister, but a future version of me, a grown-up, someone who would devote her life to describing such moments in time. This was her first word.

Hot-Air Balloon

I'M SURE MY FATHER HAS TOLD ME THAT HE LOVES ME. MAYBE WHEN I was a baby. He might have leaned over my crib, tickled one of my pea-size toes, and whispered those three enormous and compact words.

It's hard to picture Zeke doing this, though. He was twenty-two when I was born, and had the same sickening fear of babies that most men in their twenties feel. I can imagine him looking at me with tenderness, while out of the corner of his eye he was mapping every available exit.

"I love you."

He must have said these words to me in my sentient years. Maybe when I had a fever, or early on Christmas morning? On my first day of school? After I said it to him first? I am sure it has happened. It must have. I just can't remember a single time.

MY LEAST FAVORITE WORD in the English language is *avuncular*. My stomach sours whenever it appears in print. I picture a gleaming scythe swinging out of nowhere and quietly, efficiently slicing off an arm, an ear, and a chunk of my scalp. Like it was easy. Like it was nothing.

The men and women I called Uncle and Auntie were not always related to me by blood, unless you consider the needle-sharing of pre-

HIV America to be an authentic rite of kinship. Cokehead women with feathered hair christened me their niece and invited me to serve as flower girl in their weddings. Their husbands and boyfriends took me to McDonald's once in a while, and this, in my world, signified the intimacy of flesh and blood. Inevitably in relationships like these, some significant amount of money goes missing, a bag of dope is not fully paid for or paid back or picked up. I'd hear my mother screaming on the phone, and then these Aunties and Uncles would disappear. Like dandelions, a new pair would pop up around my mother's coffee table, just as wild-eyed and shaky as their predecessors. They were no better or worse than my mother's real-life siblings, so when they told me they loved me I felt compelled to love them back.

The man I called Uncle Vic had long tanned arms and every inch of them was covered with tattoos. Spiders and oil derricks and fire-breathing dragons. He had gotten them young, and their colors had already begun to fade when I first met him. He'd come to Massachusetts from one of those square-shaped states out West, where the clouds are bigger than East Coast cities. He was married to my mother's friend Lucy, a fearsome, raw-boned woman with stringy blond hair so long that she could sit on it. Uncle Vic quit school after the eighth grade, left home at fourteen, and from then on worked long, hard hours at jobs only men of his size, strength, and lack of education will do. He had a way with animals both wild and domestic. There wasn't a dog he couldn't tame, a mouse he couldn't catch. Aunt Lucy said that Vic could reach into a beehive without getting stung, but I wonder now if that was actually true or something she made up because she loved him.

It was love at first sight, he told me. And it was a secret. He would talk about it only when we were alone. Although sometimes, in a crowd, surrounded by the people we both pretended were our family, he couldn't stop himself from kneeling down and whispering, "I love you," into my ear.

The stink of beer resurfaced in a warm belch. The whiskers of his mustache scraped against my neck. If I linger too long in the reptilian stem of my brain, I can smell him right next to me now.

Pain, nausea, terror, humiliation—none of this was worse than the shameful precision with which dread had consorted with my most aching desire: I would have jumped on top of an open fire to be noticed, to be chosen, to win a precious minute of someone's attention. Uncle Vic gave that to me, and now I was being burned alive.

It was wrong—I'm sure he knew this. Legally, morally, and biologically. Grown-ups aren't supposed to find comfort inside the body of a child. But that doesn't change the essential fact: Vic was a man undeniably in love. When he looked at me I could see in his eyes that he was terrified, not of jail or lynching but of the much more harrowing possibility of rejection. For a split second he would seem smaller than me, and I felt more sorry for him than afraid.

I THINK IT WAS summer.

Sometime before then—a span of days that I couldn't measure accurately in my mind, nor can I now—I walked into my mother's apartment and found my dad on top of her, choking and thrashing her. I remember thinking it was her fault, and somehow mine as well, that there was something inside my mother and me—a howl or maybe a look—that made certain men lose their minds.

I wanted to go away. I would have gone anywhere, with anyone. As it happened, my mother's entire circle of family and friends was going on a big camping trip to Vermont, so she sent me along. Kathi didn't want to come. She had recently fallen in love with the cab-driver who would become my stepfather, and she was glad to have a week with him all to herself.

My aunts and uncles rented campground plots along a steep majestic gorge. As we set up the tents and trailers that first day, a shock of yellow peeked above the tree line. It crested, rising slowly like the sun, and revealed itself as a giant hot-air balloon. All my aunts got out their cameras, my uncles raised their beers up to the sky, and I waved at the tiny dots of people inside the basket, wondering if they could see me.

My cousins and I roamed the campground all day long, fishing and swimming and fighting with one another. The aunts and uncles hung around their campsites eating chips and onion dip and drinking cases of beer. Around dusk that first night my cousins all drifted back to their parents, and I started to panic. Where was I going to sleep?

I knew that I didn't want to camp anywhere near Aunt Lucy. She never ate anything but apples and had one lazy eye that made her look as dangerous as she actually was. Certifiable, we called Lucy behind her back. She was the kind of woman who hit babies. I had seen this with my own eyes. At the time, it seemed as indulgent to protest as it does to poeticize now; these are simply things that happened in our world. Everyone was terrified of her—men, women, and children alike. I was riding shotgun with Lucy once when a cop pulled her over for running a stop sign. "Ma'am, are you aware—" the police officer began. If he said anything else, I didn't hear it. Aunt Lucy started screaming as if she were in the throes of demonic possession. The word *scream* really doesn't capture a voice like hers. Think of the sound you would hear rising from the trenches of Ypres. The screech of virgins summoned to Mount Pelée. What came from Medea's mouth when she realized that she was now all alone.

"Aaaaaaaiiiiyyyyeeeeeee! Who do you think you are?"

She accused the police officer of pedophilia and cannibalism, shrieking so loudly that the cop jumped away from her window, stuttered a warning, and jogged back trembling to his cruiser.

When I was left alone at Lucy's house, she would tell me sick and twisted stories. "Did you hear?" she asked me one day. "The swans that nest in your river were butchered. All of them. Shred to pieces. The police found machetes near their bodies."

"Machetes?" I wondered. "Do we have those in Danvers?"

"You don't believe me?" she screamed. Her lazy eye lolled in its socket as though unhinged. "You think I'm a liar! Go look it up in the paper if you don't think it's true!"

Of course she had thrown away the paper and there was no mention of murdered swans on the TV news that night. I read my library book silently in Lucy's living room until my mother came to get me. On the car ride home, I told Mum what Auntie said about the swans.

"Lucy should have been a writer," Kathi said. "Nothing real, mind you. Not books. But the *National Enquirer* or something like that. With an imagination like hers, she could make a fortune."

Lucy was insane, and her husband was in love with me. It would have been safer if I slept alone on the precipice of the gorge. I remember stopping systematically at each of my relatives' campsites, hovering around their fires, waiting for someone to invite me to stay. Night falls faster in the woods. I watched with a leaden feeling as daylight drained from the sky. The serrated edges of treetops turned from green to gold and then, in a heartbeat, they disappeared. Now there was only darkness, the smell of fire, and the sound of shrill invisible birds. I ran to Aunt Sandy's trailer. Sandy was my favorite aunt, because she was the only adult I knew who didn't swear, and she spent her free time preserving fruit and baking pies. Mum claimed that Sandy had been a professional model in her teen years—a spread in a bridal magazine, I think. Like any story Kathi told me, there's a fifty percent chance that it's true, but I've never seen the pictures. What I remember clearly was my mother's proud invocation of her: "Your Auntie Sandy was pretty enough to marry money." This was the highest honor a woman could aspire to in my family.

Sandy's modeling career never took off, and the rich husband never arrived. She married a moody alcoholic, whom my mother described as "scantily employed," and became an overweight housewife who knowingly wrote bad checks at the local grocery store. Growing up, I was oblivious of Sandy's failures. Like my mother and everyone else in our family, I'd fallen for my aunt's high cheekbones, her nursery-school voice, those moist, buttery cookies always cooling on the stove.

"Please let me sleep here tonight." I clamped myself to Sandy's hip.

"What's wrong with you?" She peeled me off her like a wet sock. "Why are you always crying?"

"I just want to stay with you."

Did Sandy know what a pedophile Uncle Vic was? I can't be sure. My mother knew, as did others in our family; it was one of the many open secrets I overheard the women whispering about—sometimes not whispering at all—in the kitchens of my youth. A fact like that would seem hard to ignore, until you consider the human mind's most maladaptive feat of intelligence: we have a remarkable ability to believe our own lies. Denial and the desire to self-destruct are elemental cousins; mining one yields the other in equal proportion. In a family like ours, instincts like these—to hurt and to lie, reflexively first, then extensively in consequence—are so powerful that you can take them for granted as easily as, say, the lungs' ability to continue breathing when the rest of the body is fast asleep.

I remember unambiguous cries for help, and the cloud of cognitive dissonance that followed—no one did anything, no one said anything, nothing happened, nothing would change. Why? Maybe it was a warped interpretation of *omertà,* the Sicilian code of silence. Maybe everyone was afraid that if they reported Vic to the authorities, Lucy the Certifiable would try to get revenge, and the police would come knocking on *their* doors to break *their* families apart, too. There exists a nuanced arms race among those in the lowest echelon of society, a system of threats and reprisals that follows this script: *If you report me to Child Services, I'll report you for welfare fraud; if you report me to Welfare, I'll report your husband for selling pot. . . .* And so on. After all, not one member of my extended family had what you could call a model home.

Maybe Aunt Sandy was just overwhelmed with her own family troubles that night. Maybe she simply didn't think about me and where I would be sleeping.

"There's too many of us already," she said. "We don't have room for you."

I walked back to Aunt Lucy and Uncle Vic's campsite. What happened next had happened to me before and would happen a few more times until I got a little older. If I do my best mental gymnastics, I can sometimes convince myself it was a rite of initiation, a vestige of the ancient world that the rest of us pretend doesn't exist. An unholy First Communion, a sacrifice of innocence for some greater spiritual good, an act of random, senseless animal lust, a divinely inspired transgression. . . .

I've tried so many ways to make sense of my experience. Obliteration was the one that worked best. Pretend it never happened at all.

It didn't happen. It didn't happen. It didn't happen. It didn't happen. It didn't happen. It didn't happen. It didn't happen. It didn't happen. It didn't happen. It didn't happen. It didn't happen. It didn't happen. It didn't happen. It didn't happen. It didn't happen. It didn't happen.

Until one day it really didn't happen.

I don't remember many of the details now. But that can happen to any memory, toxic or not. If you can remember anything, it's already wrong. The image or event has changed, just as you have—minutely, chemically, through the passage of time between then and now. Something happens to you, and then it's gone. It becomes a memory that becomes shrapnel. Shards of experience still hot with life singe the brain wherever they happen to get embedded. Sometimes I swear I can feel the precise location of my memories like warm, tingling splinters under my scalp. Pictures with no sound, feelings with no pictures, the lost and found, mostly lost.

There are times when these memories, distilled into words and uttered in my own voice, sound so strange to me—*it didn't happen*—that I begin to doubt everything from the laws of gravity to the spelling of my own name.

MY MOTHER SHOWED UP at the campground a few days later in a Checker cab with her new boyfriend, Michael. The cab was a late model from the seventies, one of the last of its kind ever made in America. Michael had planned to retire the car from the road, but my mother rescued it from the junkyard. She drove the Checker around in circles, showing it off.

"This is the car Nikki will ride to the church on her wedding day," she bragged. She'd already had it painted white in preparation. The car would survive another couple of months before it went the way of every other vehicle she tried to own. My mother and her cars—it was always a doomed, unrequited love.

Kathi stepped grandly out of her big white boat. "I'm getting a hotel room" were the first words that came from her mouth. Mum hated camping. It reminded her too much of my competitive, outdoorsy father, who is famous for dragging his women and children on long hikes that he times with a stopwatch. My mother was driven mad by more than thirty minutes in nature. "The trees are nice, but after a while I just want to take a long, hot shower and order room service," she said, flicking her cigarette into the campfire. She ate the s'mores I made for her, then started gathering her things to leave. It was clear she was going to glide away in that huge white car and leave me behind. I panicked, started crying, complained about my chronic stomachache, which, for some reason, always aroused her sympathy.

"Nikki's sick, Michael. You mind driving us all back to Danvers?"

"No problem," he said, and grabbed a case of beer for the road.

We stopped for gas on the ride home. It was dark by then and the lights of the gas station were glowing a bilious green. When Michael got out to pump, my mother turned around in the seat and began gushing to me. "He loves me, Nikki. And he loves you, too! He told me he did. You know he'd buy you anything you want. Just ask him." She leaned her head out the window and said to Michael, "Honey, buy her a prize." Then to me, "Anything you want. He won't say no to you. He loves you so much!"

I pointed to the cashier's vestibule, where a strand of little stuffed unicorns with clasping feet was hanging on a plastic ribbon in the window. Michael got back in and gave me the unicorn. I clamped it to my finger and waved it around weakly. I tried to smile but I couldn't. Kathi turned away with a disappointed expression.

"She said she loves you," my mother told Michael. "She won't say it to you out loud because she's shy, but she loves you."

I thought, If she says the word *love* one more time, I'm going to throw up.

As Michael drained can after can of Budweiser, the big Checker cab swerved gently in and out of the lane. I watched my mother's reflection in the window. She was smiling dreamily to herself and singing along to the radio.

"Ashes to ashes, funk to funky. We know Major Tom's a junkie."

At some point she turned around and asked me if I'd had fun in Vermont.

"That hot-air-balloon festival looked cool. Did you get to go for a ride in one?"

"No," I said. A lie. It escaped from my mouth like a puff of smoke, something real, something visible, but only for a moment.

I had gone up in a hot-air balloon. Uncle Vic had bought us a ride, and this is what I remember: Green mountains, silent and immense. The thin blue vein of a river twisting between them. Giant balloons of all colors floating dumbly across the sky. Above my head the intermittent blast of fire; below me tiny evergreens, tiny buildings, tiny people—everything far away and unreal. But beautiful, and so painful, and then something more than either of those things. Just below the surface of the world, a great mystery was thrumming with the dim insistence of a pulse. It was much bigger than this moment, bigger than my uncle, bigger than my whole life, and I was lucky to be alive for even five minutes and feel it.

Except, I can't possibly have held such a thought in my mind. The only thing I remember for sure was hovering above the earth, trying my hardest to forget.

Lonesome

WHEN I WAS A KID, THE MOST POPULAR BOOKS FOR GIRLS WAS a series called *The Baby-sitters Club*. There are around two hundred novels in total, all about a girl named Stacey and her vast network of best friends who work with her in a weirdly noncompetitive babysitting collective. Stacey is pretty, athletic, and entrepreneurial, the kind of girl who is overjoyed to get her first menstrual period. Nothing in the known world can get Stacey down. Not when the rival gymnastics team threatens to win the trophy (they will trip over their hubris in the finals, obviously), not even her parents' sensible, compassionate divorce. ("Now I have *two* bedrooms to decorate!" our heroine might squeal.)

But Stacey is no immortal. Like the rest of us, she has an Achilles' heel, and hers lurks inside every cupcake that comes her way. Little Stacey, you see, is deathly diabetic, a fact that she seems to forget at the climax of every *Baby-sitters* novel.

I read half a dozen of these books even though I hated them. I was afraid that if I didn't, I would miss out on some arcane girl knowledge that the kids at school could use against me. The plots are formulaic and predictable. There is always a moment when Stacey goes to a birthday party and eats herself into diabetic shock, followed by the inevitable rescue, a trip to the hospital, and an outpouring of love from family, friends, and one cute boy whose devotion to her is as sincere as it is chaste.

By this point in the book, I truly hoped Stacey would die. I wanted to execute her personally. Set her hair on fire. Hold her face underwater until the bubbles stopped. I hated her. I hated everyone.

I DIDN'T HAVE MANY friends growing up; then I hit puberty and things got even worse. Here begins my angry phase, the self-centered, quietly homicidal years, that special hiccup of time between my first bra and my first joint. Fortunately for my peers, I spent most of my free time during childhood and early adolescence sleeping. This is no exaggeration. In fourth grade I discovered that I could knock myself out with prescription antihistamines. I would come home from school, flick on the TV, breeze through my homework while watching *Donahue,* then pop a couple of pills during the opening credits of *The Oprah Winfrey Show.* Making it that far into the day without any emotional pyrotechnics from my mother seemed like a real victory, and I would reward myself with a nice, deep, chemically induced nap. A few hours later, I would wake up and microwave a frozen lasagna to eat in bed while watching horrible network sitcoms. It's possible that I hated the characters on these TV shows even more than the girls in *The Baby-sitters Club.* Yet I watched my sitcoms religiously. Even if I was engrossed in a book, I would leave the television on in the background. I didn't know how to face the night without it. What would happen to me alone in my room, alone with my thoughts?

Many nights, if my mother was rehearsing her next performance as Medea, or the networks were in reruns, I would take another allergy pill after dinner and pass out in my school uniform. Why bother taking it off? I'd just have to put it on again in the morning. If only there were a button I could push to fast-forward me into the future, I used to think, then I'd be an old lady with everything already behind me. I had no idea what *everything* was or even looked like. I just knew that I wanted it to be over. Life felt trapped in slow motion, childhood was going to last forever, and I would always be bracing myself, squeezing my pencil so tightly my knuckles turned white, grinning and bearing, never knowing when or if it would ever be safe to relax.

DESPITE ALL THIS, I started adolescence as a minor hero. In sixth grade I got boobs. They have since shrunk significantly, now sad puckered little things, like partially deflated balloons the day after a birthday party. A decade of yo-yo dieting will do that. But their debut was sudden, disproportionate, and newsworthy, as eighty percent of the girls at school were still flat-chested. The few girls who could fill a bra quickly formed a clique and recruited me to join. It was a very calculated, kind of ingenious, preteen maneuver: the deliberate consolidation of power. As far as I could tell, boobs were the only things we had in common; but for a brief period I walked with the alpha girls, floating high on the fumes of inclusion. Still an insatiable overachiever, I was always waving my hand hysterically in the air—*Please, please call on me! I know the answer! Pick me!* The girls in my clique tolerated this for a while. They already had a slutty girl, a rich girl, and a jock girl in their ranks, so a brainy one rounded out our portfolio.

By eighth grade Mum got ambitious. She had her heart set on a college scholarship, though college was still four years away, and began prodding me to get serious about extracurriculars. "Good grades aren't enough these days," she said. "You'll need to start doing volunteer work and play a team sport."

She signed me up to start babysitting little kids at a domestic-violence shelter. Class president proved to be an easy win and carried no real responsibilities. For a sport, I picked cheerleading, because, at the very least, it spared me the indignity of having to use a mouth guard. Our school was tiny, and every girl who tried out got a spot on the team. As we were all equally inept at back handsprings, the role of captain was chosen based on a one-page essay entitled "Why I Should Be Captain of the Cheerleaders." On the second day of practice, the coaches passed out sheets of paper and told us that we had twenty minutes to write.

I looked around at all the girls spread out on the gymnasium floor, with their sparkly notebooks and pens, and almost felt sorry for them. It wasn't fair, really, how devastated they were about to be. I toyed with the idea of humbly withdrawing from the contest. Then I cracked my knuckles, licked my lips, and scribbled out the Gettysburg Address of cheerleading.

That winter I was chosen for the role of the Virgin Mary in the annual Christmas pageant. Since this was the highest honor a girl at my school could achieve, the person who would play Mary became a topic of speculation at least a year in advance. Long brown hair and a simple majority vote among fellow students were the only criteria; it was essentially a popularity contest that took into account your everlasting soul. I tried my hardest to accept the role with the grace and poise befitting the Mother of God, but I had always been a bad winner.

Loud mouth, straight A's, and boobs—I had no idea how or for what these things were exploited, only that they attracted all kinds of attention from men and women, girls and boys. Aunt Sandy once scowled at me in my bathing suit as I prepared to cannonball into her pool, and said to my mother, "That's not right. She's too young to be that busty," as though my body were somehow my fault. So it was only a matter of time before the witch hunt, before someone came after me.

And they did. My classmates and some of their mothers and even some of the teachers. *Who does she think she is? Her mother is that bleach-blond you-know-what. They never go to church. Her mother didn't even come to the Christmas pageant.* (Because, she told me, she was bored to tears by singing schoolchildren and would rather stay at work and make money.) Clearly, my mother and I weren't in the same league as these whispering middle-aged women and their scrawny-legged scions. How dare I have the things that belonged to their girls? How dare I win, and worse, win everything?

The beginning of the end fell on picture day in eighth grade. Because we wore uniforms, picture day was a big deal, one of only four days throughout the year in which we showed up at school in normal clothes. My mother woke up uncharacteristically early that morning so that she could blow-dry and straighten my hair. I wouldn't let that woman near my eyes with a sharpened eyeliner pencil, but I let her brush rouge onto my cheeks ("Subtle, Mum! Please be subtle!") and a little mascara, which she let me apply myself. Kathi and I had put an outfit together the night before: black cotton sweater, jean shorts, black tights, and a pair of brown leather ankle boots with a tiny heel.

"How do I look?" I asked Mum.

"With those boots?" she said. "Killer."

Just before I left the house my mother added a final touch, a black beaded necklace with a black cross in the center.

My homeroom teacher was Mrs. Collins, a middle-aged prune with a helmet of stiff, prematurely gray hair. Earlier in the year I'd spotted a pack of cigarettes in her desk drawer, and I shot her a knowing look. "I thought you smelled familiar!" I joked. She didn't laugh, and a mortal enmity was born. Like all people who dislike me, Mrs. Collins became the center of my universe. Her opinion meant everything, and I would have sawed off my left arm if it meant that she would scribble "Good" in red pen at the top of my papers.

I think it was the black cross that did me in. Mrs. Collins looked me up and down, then quickly got up from her desk. She grabbed me by the arm and pulled me into the girls' bathroom. I didn't resist or even question her. I was too afraid. I had never seen Mrs. Collins touch any of her students before. I assumed that she was having a Lizzie Borden breakdown, about to murder us all one by one, starting with me.

"*What* are you wearing?" Mrs. Collins said once the lavatory door swung shut.

What was the right answer to that question? For the first time, I didn't know. I stared into my teacher's eyes and burst into tears. More questions followed, more bumbling tears, until the inevitable:

"Did your mother see how you dressed yourself this morning?"

"Yes."

Many women leave their reproductive years with wisdom and dignity, but not everyone crosses the threshold so willingly. Those women become the warty hags of our childhood fairy tales, the

big-nosed, green-skinned witches with ovens equipped to broil a nu-
bile thirteen-year-old girl. Envy is like oxygen to these miserable gor-
gons. They gargle with lamb's blood and spit out napalm. I know all
this firsthand because, almost every year, a Hydra like this resurfaced
in the form of a schoolteacher. Mrs. Collins was the meanest of
them all.

She called in another teacher, and then the school principal. The
three women stood in the bathroom shaking their heads, clicking
their tongues at me, literally *tsking*. They never said *prostitute, trol-
lop,* or *hussy,* though I'm sure all of these and more crossed their
minds; as Catholic-school professionals, they used the words *disgrace* and *shameful* instead. Someone procured a pair of gray sweatpants, and I was told to take off my shorts and put them on. Then
Mrs. Collins marched me back to class, to thirty pairs of eyes waiting feverishly for our return, and everyone got in line according to
height. In the pictures, which I tore up the second I saw them, my
eyes are small and red and my smile is tired.

That same day, Melanie Higgins was wearing a spandex skirt that
looked as if it had been painted on her skin. Krista McDonald's bra
was so padded that it laughed in the face of reality. Amanda Di Lo-
renzo looked like a midget Tammy Faye Bakker, with her blue eye
shadow and clumped blue mascara. The shorts I had on were neither
scandalous nor ripped. My tights were opaque, and the sweater's
only offense was its color; it had a high neck that grazed my collar-
bone and fell loosely to my waist. These were the points my mother
made when she came in the next day to raise hell.

"My daughter has never even kissed a boy, and you people made
her feel like a whore," she shouted. It didn't help our cause much, not
with all the cleavage Mum was showing as she said these things.

Shortly after picture day, my classmates decided to impeach me as
their president. They had discussed it all behind my back and elected
a few representatives to broach the issue during social studies. I'd
never thought much of my classmates' intellect, so when this happened I was shocked and slightly impressed. The little plebeians had

organized. Our teacher, Mrs. King, was a frail, pretty sparrow, easily bowled over by a roomful of hateful thirteen-year-olds. She didn't know what to do, so she made me wait in the hall while the rest of the students discussed my failings in a quorum and then, in democratic fashion, voted me out.

"Why are they doing this to you?" Mrs. King asked when she returned to the hall to deliver the class's verdict. ("Not *totally* unanimous," she offered as a consolation.) She was very tall, so she had to bend at the hips to meet me eye to eye, and when she finally looked at me she began to cry.

"I don't understand, Nikki. How can they be so—so cruel?"

These questions weren't purely rhetorical, I realized. Mrs. King actually wanted me to explain them to her.

For my entire life up to that point, school had been a six-hour respite from home. There was a reassuring pattern to every period, day, week, and semester. I understood exactly what was expected of me and could deliver it in return. I knew the right answers. Even if my teachers didn't like me—and I sensed that many of them didn't—I got concrete validation in test scores and letter grades. Now life at St. Mary's was no better than it was at home.

The impeachment took place on a Monday, a night that I slept at my father's, and as I walked to his house after school that day I decided to kill myself as soon as everyone went to bed. I tried to explain to my dad and Carla what had happened at school, but either they didn't believe me or they didn't fully understand. I took my diary to the backyard and wrote a poem about the moon, then swallowed a combination of allergy pills and generic-brand aspirin. I think now part of me must have understood that if I'd swallowed the kinds of pills stocked at my mother's house I most definitely would have died. Thank God, it all ended ingloriously with a lot of vomit. I didn't even fall into a coma, which was my ultimate goal—to lie like Sleeping Beauty on a hospital bed made of Lucite until a handsome college admissions officer woke me up with a letter of acceptance, a scholarship, and a kiss.

After a boring couple of hours in the Salem Hospital ER, I was interviewed by a therapist whose nametag read "Leesah." For forty-five minutes, this woman and I stared at each other in tense silence.

"Has anyone ever touched you inappropriately?"

"No."

"Have you ever been hit?"

"No."

"Are you afraid for your safety at home . . . ?"

Leesah discharged me. I got one day off to watch game shows and soap operas at my dad's house, then I went back to school and life as usual. Everyone knew that I had botched a suicide—my mother's big mouth made sure of that—and I felt even more humiliated. Yet I was still acting my part as captain of the cheerleaders. I must have been a gloomy sight even before all this happened. With my thick black eyebrows and the dark circles under my eyes, there was no amount of ribbon or glitter that could make me appear very cheerful. Our primary purpose was to support the boys' basketball team, which lost nearly every game that year, and sometimes compete against other girls in cheering competitions, where we always came in second to last.

"We suck so much, sucking is, like, our only superlative," I said to myself aloud in the locker room.

Soon after the presidential coup d'état, I was kicked off the squad. The mother of my co-captain had orchestrated it. Her best friend's daughter took my place. Around the same time, national news broke the story of a woman in Texas who tried to have someone killed so that her daughter could be captain of the cheerleading squad.

"Fuck!" my mother said. "Nikki, that could have been you!"

I spent a lot of time that year lying on the floor of my bedroom listening to Nirvana and the Cure. I produced a staggering number of poems. Most of them rhymed, though I was wont to write little prose pieces, like this one I found in my diary:

I know that beneath the silence is the sound of blood. That means the quiet is a lie. There is another world, the inner

*world of our bodies, made of millions of microscopic martyrs
who work endlessly to keep us alive even when we, the totality
of their efforts, want so badly for it to stop, for it to end, for us
to die.*

In order to maintain their social position, the circle of friends I'd
acquired had to dump me. They had their eyes trained on higher
stakes these days anyway—high-school boys with driver's licenses.
Through what I imagine to be a series of very ardent, clumsy hand
jobs, one of them convinced their new car-driving friends to stalk
and harass me at my house, prank-call me at all hours, and leave
threatening messages on our answering machine.

"They said things, Nikki, I don't even want to tell you," my
mother said with a shudder.

Though, a minute later, she did.

"They said they were going to rape and kill you and leave your
body for me to find! I was so nice to your friends." My mother
pouted. "I can't believe they would turn on me like this."

Reports of young girls being raped and murdered were always on
the evening news. In light of everything else that was going on, it
didn't seem impossible that I could be next. I didn't feel safe living at
my mother's house anymore, where the trill of the telephone made
my pulse race and the sound of tires on the gravel had me ducking
away from the windows. Nonna had just survived her first heart attack. Under the pretense that my grandmother needed my help to
recover, I moved into her apartment next door.

WHEN MY MOTHER WAS a little girl, my grandmother tended bar at a
place called the Tack Room. "I was raised in that barroom," Kathi
said of her childhood. It was an unfortunate necessity, because Nonna's husband, Mike, had left her for another woman years before they
legally divorced, and she couldn't afford to choose between raising
her children and earning an income. One of Nonna's sisters had married a man who owned a stable of racehorses, and my grandmother

took up side work running numbers for him. Rita wasn't afraid to move a bag of dope when she needed the money, and she taught her most intelligent and enterprising daughter, Kathi, how to do the same. The critical difference between this mother-and-daughter pair was that my mother grew up to be a narcotic omnivore, while her mother remained staunchly sober. My grandmother refused to touch alcohol and never developed any personal interest in the drugs she occasionally sold; she was, ironically, disgusted by anyone who did. "No-good fuckin' losers!" she said, referring to such people, which included almost all of her relatives by both blood and marriage.

My grandmother was just as crazy as everyone else in our gene pool, but I had rightfully identified her as the most trustworthy person among us. Since I was old enough to balance on two feet, I would toddle to where she lived next door and she would look at me as no one else in our family did—as if I was really there.

I had always loved to read, and as I got older my appetite for fiction grew in ways I didn't know how to meet. By the time I turned eleven, I'd ripped through every Agatha Christie novel I could find in both the school and the town library. I knew there was something better out there, but I didn't know what it was or how to find it, so I asked my mother to buy me nothing but books for my birthday. Kathi came home with a stack of Disney books with huge illustrations and one dull sentence per page.

"Thanks, Mum." I pretended to smile as I opened the books, inwardly ashamed for us both. When she was high, she often forgot how old I was, and shopping was one of those chores made more bearable by Percocet or cocaine.

Later in the week, I walked over to my grandmother's house for my birthday dinner. She'd decided my present that year would be a trip to the bookstore, where I could pick out whatever I wanted. I chose the complete works of William Shakespeare. I liked the heft of the volume, the black leather cover, and the gold paint on the edge of the pages. As my grandmother worked on dinner, I sat on her porch and read *Romeo and Juliet,* because it was the most famous and I thought it would be the easiest to understand.

"They weren't really in love!" I shouted to Nonna through the screen door. She was frying disks of breaded summer squash in olive oil, our favorite snack. "They didn't even know each other! They're just young kids and wicked overly emotional."

"Everyone always thinks it's this big love story," she yelled back.

"It's not! It's much better than that!"

I heard my grandmother laughing above the crackle of oil, felt a warm breeze swirl around me. The river looked like a wrinkled sheet of silk, blue and green and black and white. If we get to keep anything of this life after we die, that afternoon is what I would choose.

Growing up, I could wander over to my grandmother's house at any hour of the day or night, and she would always get up to cook something for me. We would sit together in her kitchen, listening to Billie Holiday on the AM radio station she loved, and stuff ourselves silly on loaves of warm bread. Nonna was a shrieking harpy to her own children, but she truly enjoyed the genetic remove of being a grandmother.

"Don-ah look atta my granddaughter! Oh, please! Don-ah look! She eez homely and stunata!" she would wail in public, holding her hand over my face. It was a trick of advertising in reverse that she had learned from her own Sicilian grandmother, who believed that Gypsies were always lurking around the corner, scouting young blood to steal into their clan. Publicly denouncing your offspring as damaged goods sent a message to these Gypsies that they'd be better off kidnapping someone else's child. If I'd had a tail, it would have wagged hysterically whenever Nonna hid my face and told strangers at the supermarket that I was an ugly simpleton. If someone wanted to steal me, I thought, I must be a person of real value. Better still, someone wanted to protect me from being stolen.

WHEN MY MOTHER AND Michael got married, they slept in a water bed behind our living-room couch and used my bedroom closet for their clothes and other effects. The storage space of one closet wasn't nearly sufficient to contain the hoard of their boxes and trash bags.

These things piled up and blockaded the door to my bedroom so that it couldn't be shut without causing an avalanche. It was clear to everyone that our family of three needed more privacy and space, so Nonna offered to swap homes with Kathi and Michael. She moved into our little one-bedroom apartment and we took over her house at 35 Eden Glen Avenue. In the spring of 1993, my stepdad disassembled my twin bed and reassembled it in the space where the water bed once stood behind the living-room couch. Nonna was in my old bedroom, her TV blaring all day and night. The oblong teak mask that my grandfather had brought home from the Pacific after World War II hung on the wall across from my bed. I would fall asleep staring into its wooden eyes, the thick lips pressed into a bemused smile, and wonder what secrets the mask was keeping from us.

My grandmother had recently retired from her job as a kitchen aide in a hospital cafeteria. She was in her golden years now, a time she spent screaming at her television and trying to re-clog her recently shunted arteries.

"Nonna, that has a lot of cholesterol," I would say as I watched her drop an entire stick of butter into a pot of angel hair.

"Ba fangul," she shouted back. She added olive oil, salt, and a pound of crispy bacon to the pot. "Maybe I want to die!"

Nonna was very weak from her surgeries, and I enjoyed playing her nurse. I occupied myself with cleaning and other chores, keeping her to a schedule of medications, and taking her blood-sugar readings. After a triple-bypass surgery, Nonna couldn't stand longer than a few minutes or raise her arms to wash herself. We put a plastic deck chair in the shower and I would stand outside the curtain with a cloth, gently soaping her back and shampooing her hair. At thirteen I was still afraid of the dark, but I didn't flinch at the sight of my grandmother's wiry gray pubic hair, the ribbon of scar tissue from the bypass that sliced her from heart to thigh, the pink satiny coil of skin left by the mastectomy she had before I was born. It was the image of my grandmother with wet hair that I found distressing. Nonna had those fabled Sicilian follicles—thick, coarse strands of hair, each one gleaming and tough as steel wool.

Throughout my grandmother's battle with breast cancer and the course of chemotherapy, she did not lose a single strand. All five of her children corroborate this story, which leads me to believe that it might actually be true. I had always known my grandmother as a woman with a thick pouf of hair, set and curled like the typical old lady's and dyed a purplish red. Sitting in the shower with her head sopping, she looked small and meek in a way I had never imagined possible.

As with my father, I don't remember my grandmother ever saying that she loved me, but I never questioned that she did because of the names she called me—*giugiunelle* or *putan,* chickpea or whore. Terms of endearment, obviously, because she also used to call her cats these names. Nonna's cats, Balthazar and Nicodemus, were the two biggest whores we knew. They used to disappear for days. "Out whoring!" Nonna would yell as though summoning them home. When the cats finally returned, she would cook them their own dinner of liver and tripe. One of them—Balthazar, I think—contracted a feline strain of the AIDS virus. This was in the eighties, at the height of the HIV epidemic, when misinformation was rampant and everyone was paranoid about catching it from a toilet seat. There were several heroin addicts in our extended network of friends and family who were HIV positive.

"That's what he gets for being such a whore!" Nonna chastised the cat.

She would have said the same thing to any of her children had they come to her with such a diagnosis. But when her prodigal son returned mewling after a few nights on the prowl, Nonna's eyes would tear and she would fry an egg just for him.

At this point in her life my grandmother had long since given up wearing a prosthetic breast, let alone a bra. She didn't wear her dentures, comb her hair, or shave her armpits. Lisa and Donald had told me that all the kids on Eden Glen Avenue thought my grandmother was a witch. It was a natural conclusion, given her toothless, one-titted rants at the neighbors and the way she muttered angrily to herself while walking up and down the street. Jehovah's Witnesses once knocked on her door. Once. My mother and I were in the driveway next door, getting ready to go out, when we saw the two young men in crisp suits climbing the steps of her porch.

"Hold on, Nik," Mum said. "I want to watch this."

We saw them knock on her door and wait. A shriek and a curse later, they were running for their lives. Nothing could have made me prouder.

Living with Nonna had many advantages, the biggest being food. She had that Depression-era talent for making a feast out of nothing. One night I watched her take rotten, almost liquefied peppers and tomatoes from the windowsill where she'd left them to ripen. She cut off the green, fuzzy mold and fried the remaining bits in olive oil with meat and potatoes and garlic.

"That's friggin' gross, Nonna. I'm not eating it."

"*Statta zite!* You'll eat it, you *putan!*" she hollered, and banished me from the kitchen. After dinner I was licking the pan she had cooked it all in.

When I remember my grandmother now, I picture her sitting on her living-room couch, wearing a cheap cotton housedress, her one, lopsided boob drooping toward her hip, her wild, reddish hair sticking up in all directions, and the crooked smile on her face as she leans over to one side and waves her hands to divert a loud, rippling fart in my direction.

"You know, Nikki, every time a person passes gas invisible particles of shit are flying through the air!"

WHEN I HAD FINISHED with my homework and the horrible sitcoms I watched, Nonna would transplant herself to the living-room couch so that we could watch TV together until one of us fell asleep. We stayed up late into the night watching old movies that my grandmother called "pictures." The spring I lived with her we watched *The Pit and the Pendulum,* the entire *Shogun* series, and Alex Haley's *Roots.* Several other movies I sometimes think we dreamed. If imaginations can be inherited, mine certainly was, because Nonna and I had an identical subconscious. Those months when we lived together were full of magical projection. It was uncanny the way we were always finding bits of our darkest desires being enacted on the screen. There was one movie about a lake in rural North America infested with piranhas. As shoals of bloodthirsty fish shredded the limbs of teenagers from a nearby summer camp, I imagined the kids at St. Mary's being devoured.

"I'm rooting for the piranhas," Nonna said, as though she could hear my thoughts.

In another of our late-night B-movie horror shows, nuclear fallout causes the few surviving men and women to roam the scorched earth with painful, lumpy mutations growing out of their bodies. "We deserve a lot worse than that, after the way we've treated this planet," Nonna said in disgust.

Even nature programs revealed to us the brutal world as we recognized it: sharks leaving flesh wounds as part of the courtship ritual, procreation by gang rape, and, for the finale, intrauterine cannibalism! Shakespeare couldn't have done a finer job.

EVENTUALLY I MOVED BACK home with my mother. I became a teenager and discovered sex—truly my gateway drug. Nonna was watching TV next door as always, though I went to see her less and less. My life was full of boys. I no longer needed the company of a crazy old lady. But I still called often to check on her.

"Hello, Nonna, it's me. Just calling to make sure you haven't died yet. Have you? Okay. Bye." I was showing off for some guy, trying to prove how dark and fascinating I was.

The truth was that my grandmother and I talked about death often. "It's gonna happen! To me, to you. We're gonna die." Nonna loved to remind me when I was a trembling little kid afraid of my own shadow. She took me by the shoulders and gently shook me.

"Listen to me," she said. "Only a moron would be scared."

———

THE LAST TIME I saw my grandmother, I was an eighteen-year-old college freshman. My mother had turned her life around, financially at least, and for the first time we were confronted with the burden of surplus income. Kathi was of the mind that her money possessed the ability to fly out the window like a colony of bats leaving a cave at dusk, and she was determined to spend what she had before that could happen. It would be allegory in neon, this reversal of fortune, a spectacular failure about to burn the horizon like a hot summer sunset. I had to act fast if I was going to take advantage of my mother's temporary boom, so I charged a round-trip ticket to Amsterdam and a two-month Eurail pass on her American Express card. It would be my first time leaving the country, traveling without a "grown-up," traveling somewhere farther than Disney World. There were many firsts ahead of me, and I was so excited and self-absorbed and adolescent that I hardly remembered anyone in the world existed besides me. I am ashamed to admit that my mother actually had to remind me to go next door and say goodbye.

I knocked twice and walked in, as was my custom, and Nonna began shouting at me: "What are you doing here? I told your mother not to send you over! Get out of here!"

I started to say goodbye, and Nonna burst into tears. "I didn't want to see you," she shrieked and took me into her arms. "Now get! I told you—go!"

I hugged and kissed her and said goodbye. We both knew it would be the last time.

I wrote to my grandmother from Italy, a place we'd always dreamed about visiting together, but by then it was too late. I took a train from Rome to Champéry, Switzerland, where I crashed at the apartment of a rich college friend. We drank bottles of scotch, smoked potent Dutch hash, and had stoned, pretentious conversations with other backpackers about Life and Art. One morning, while I was walking to the market to buy cigarettes and milk, I saw a bright red biplane doing tricks in the air: loop-the-loops and flips and turns. The plane looked like a toy in the wide blue sky, like a child playing, or the spirit of a child, or the spirit of an old body suddenly returned to youth. In an instant, I knew: my grandmother was dead and she had come to say goodbye to me.

"Bye, Nonna." I waved at the little plane, and shortly afterward it flew away.

I walked back to the apartment, poured a glass of scotch, and made a collect call to Zeke. My mother had made a rule that I call her at least three times a week. During these conversations she provoked hysterical, transatlantic fights. She'd been on an especially manic swing since I'd left Italy. Something was clearly going on, and she wasn't telling me. I figured, correctly, that my father, whom I hardly ever called even when we were in the same country, would be caught off guard and couldn't lie.

"Nonna's dead, isn't she?" I asked him, and he told me that she'd had a stroke a few days ago and died in the hospital the night before.

"Don't tell your mother I told you. She's crazier than ever over all this."

Kathi tried to maintain the lie until I came home a month later. When I got back from Europe that summer each of my aunts had ransacked their mother's apartment, pillaging every memento they wanted before someone else could get her hands on it first. Gone were the large cast-iron skillets in which Nonna had cooked her best meals, her antique pasta-maker with the squeaky metal crank, all the afghans she had knitted until her eyes gave out, her small collection of costume jewelry, her large brown sunglasses with the spotted lenses that she would never clean.

"Don't bother going over there," my mother said. "My sisters— they got together without telling me and took everything. They didn't leave anything for us."

But they did. And I knew just where to look for it. Nonna had told me years ago, "You can have this when I die, but not until then." It was a certificate for good penmanship, given to my grandmother in 1941, when she was in elementary school. This scrap of yellowed paper was something she'd treasured. She'd kept it folded up in a copy of Carl Sagan's *Intelligent Life in the Universe* for decades. Sometimes she'd pull it out and show me. "I had beautiful handwriting," she'd say. "All my teachers said so." It was the only award she ever received.

I READ ONCE THAT by the time a female fetus reaches the second trimester every egg she will ever have in her life has already been formed. Bundled neatly in her tiny ovaries, these eggs will wait decades for their chance to seed the next generation. Meaning, once upon a time, before my mother was my mother, she was a helpless, hairless thing yearning to be born, and half of me was already inside her, and inside my grandmother as well.

Nonna was the only person in my family to ask me if my new stepfather "was trying to get at me." No, he wasn't. But I was haunted, nevertheless, and she knew it. One night I crossed the yard that separated our homes, walked into her apartment, and for no reason that I could explain, began to cry. A pressure was building inside me—I felt it all the time, even in moments of quiet contentment. Lying on my grandmother's couch, I folded my legs and arms into my body. I wanted to make myself as small as a seed, something tiny and weightless that could easily be carried away by the wind and lost in the world.

"You're just one of those people, Nikki," she said. "Like me. We're lonesome. That's all."

There isn't a word in the English language more beautiful than *lonesome*. Nonna's understanding of it was neither a pathology, like depression, nor a mood that comes and goes with sociable visitors. I would grow up to find that no friend, no boyfriend, not even a room full of people throwing a party just for me, could pry the lonesomeness from the body it inhabited. It was a shadow sewn to the soles of my feet, something as inexorable, dark, and magical as death. The whole world could be contained in that single word, and for me, right then, that was enough.

Gateway

————

ACCORDING TO MY DIARY, I SPENT THE FIRST DAY OF SUMMER 1993 reorganizing my bureau and closet. When that was finished, I rooted underneath the bathroom sink to find dozens of bottles of lotion and shampoo, all one-eighth full, which I married off so that I could throw away the empties. I then pulled all the towels from the bathroom cupboards and refolded them so that they would stack more efficiently. After that I scrubbed the bathtub and trimmed the brown mildewed hem of the shower curtain. When my mother discovered that I had done this with her expensive, professional-grade salon scissors, she screamed and wailed and threw the scissors at me like a deranged circus act. The rest of the day and night I watched a marathon of *Beavis and Butt-Head,* my bedroom door closed but my ears focused on the sounds of Kathi's every movement.

"Now what?" I wrote in my journal. I was thirteen going on fourteen and my handwriting was tiny and painstakingly neat.

But a miracle would occur later that summer. My mother joined a Twelve-Step recovery program for people addicted to food. Eating was the least of Kathi's addictions, but this was definitely a move in the right direction. She went to a lot of support meetings and set aside time every day to pray for serenity, courage, and wisdom. She spent so much time on the phone talking to her sugar-abstinent friends that she had less energy to yell at me. She still blew up with the force of Mount Etna, but these eruptions were significantly less frequent, and sometimes she even apologized afterward.

Her life was now full of people she met at her meetings, and that summer those women became my friends. There was a woman named Crisanne who believed the actor Kevin Costner was communicating with her through the CHECK ENGINE light on her car's dashboard. Crisanne's entire family had years ago stopped speaking to her, for their own sanity and survival, so she turned to rooms full of strangers, people like my mother, to listen patiently to her hallucinations. Too crazy to hold down a job, she lived on Social Security. At least three times a week, she ate lunch at our house. She had curly brown hair down to her shoulders and often wore her clothing inside out by accident.

"Crisanne, Honey, go fix your shirt," my mother would say between drags of her cigarette. Crisanne would laugh and babble on as though no one else was there.

"The key to dealing with her," Mum whispered to me, "is to stop listening when she gets boring. Just think of something else to entertain yourself. All her stories have a pattern. They get a little predictable. Christ, the poor kid just wants to find love."

There was another Twelve-Stepper named Beth who was blind and frail. She had stringy gray hair and the gaunt cheekbones of a glue-sniffing orphan. At most, this woman weighed eighty pounds. Wherever Beth went she had to carry a pillow, because sitting in most chairs was too painful for her bony rear. I have no idea what this woman was doing in a support group for overeaters, but my mother found her there, and Beth became a regular at our house and in our car.

That same summer my mother's husband, Michael, had bought her a used, two-toned maroon-and-white Caddy Coupe Deville. This car didn't run, it *sailed*. Kathi loved any excuse to drive it and volunteered to serve as Beth's personal chauffeur. It was part of my mother's Twelve Steps—she had to make amends for her past sins, and, as she saw it, carting this blind lady around was one of the good and selfless deeds that she owed to the universe.

"Nikki, how old do you think Beth is?" my mother asked as we waited for one of Beth's many state-subsidized assistants to help her out of her house and into our car.

"I don't know," I said. "Sixty?"

"Thirty-two!" Mum flicked her cigarette out the window and waved the smoke away from my face. "I'd rather be fat than look that old."

SUMMERS IN NEW ENGLAND are hot, but they're also merciful. A heat wave will go on for three or four days, five at the absolute most, and then, without fail, a cool rain shower will break the spell. My mother and I would sit on the porch with Nonna and watch these summer storms the way other people watched the Boston Red Sox. Black clouds rolled across the sky, the river turned the color of smoke, and the three of us sat on the picnic table like giddy witches who had summoned the thunder with the power of our thoughts. We loved nothing so much as a lightning storm. If it happened during the day, my mother would stop everything to sit and watch it. If it came at night, she'd wake me up so that we could watch it together. We'd listen to the birds scream and scatter. The wind would swell with the momentum of a symphony until it ripped open the sky.

My mother saw storms as a cause for celebration, and that summer we had a full-fledged hurricane. She got on the phone before the lines were cut and called everyone she knew to come to our porch and watch the show. "Call your friends, Nikki," she said, forgetting in her excitement that I didn't have any. When no one showed up, she was totally baffled. She'd made a large bowl of ranch dip and chopped up celery and carrots. We had hors d'oeuvres and front-row seats. Why anyone would hide indoors was beyond her.

I huddled with her on the porch, tucking my knees inside my sweatshirt to keep warm. Reeds of phragmite six feet high swept flat across the marsh. The sky and the river were the same shade of gray. Everything was silent except for the wind.

"It must look gorgeous farther out," Mum said. "Up in Gloucester . . ."

The next thing I knew we were in the car, driving into the heart of the storm. Mum followed a winding coastal road with a view of the ocean pretty much the whole way. Every now and then she veered off to the shoulder so that we could get a better look at what was happening out at sea. I rolled down the window and stuck my head out. Kathi pulled over on the peak of a rocky bluff. The waves were crashing higher than I'd ever seen in my life.

"It's spilling over the top! Onto the road!" I cried.

It did not occur to me to be afraid. I was with my mother. We were in a Cadillac. What on this small planet had the power to hurt us?

THE REST OF THAT summer was sticky and hot. A mixture of humidity and cigarette smoke left a grimy film on my skin. Sleep was impossible. I woke up every hour drenched in sweat. One morning Kathi had the brilliant idea to strip the sheets off our beds and store them in the freezer during the day. We remade our beds that night, and seven minutes later we were as hot and miserable as ever.

"These fans—they just push the hot air around," my mother complained.

We went for long, aimless drives to cool ourselves off. Sometimes we'd invite Crisanne, who was always asking if we could stop somewhere and get ice cream. We'd pick up Beth and her pillow and take her to do errands. Beth had a guide dog named Kenny, a handsome, reserved German shepherd who sometimes came with us on our drives. I wasn't allowed to pat him—no one was—but his quiet, dutiful presence was something I could feel no matter how out of reach he was. Beth always spoke to him in a dissatisfied tone of voice and often threatened to get rid of him. Then, one day, she did.

"Where did he go? Can we find him and adopt him?" I begged my mother. "How can you be friends with a person who would do something like that?"

"There but for the grace of God go I," my mother said.

"What does that even mean?"

My mother had no answer. She often spouted the dogma of her

Twelve Steps without doing much to substantiate it. One of the steps required her to write down on paper an exhaustive list of all the people who had ever done her wrong. She filled several spiral notebooks with the details of her resentments, railing against everyone who had ever hurt her, including me.

"Nikki, you're incredibly abusive to me," she said in a calm voice after completing a long afternoon of writing. "I want you to know that I'm no longer going to accept that kind of treatment from anyone, least of all you."

"What? What?" I was choking on sobs, gasping for air.

"I wrote you a long letter about it."

"Can I read it?"

"No," she said. "I tore it into little pieces and threw it away. You should write me a letter, too, Honey. Then rip it up and throw it away. You won't believe how good it feels."

MY MOTHER WAS WORKING as a manicurist at the time. She had a table at a small beauty salon in Beverly Farms where the clients were all wealthy, blue-blooded housewives, including, she reported proudly, some bona-fide Saltonstalls, the preeminent Massachusetts dynasty who'd been running the state in one way or another for more than three hundred years. These old-money New England WASPs absolutely loved my mother, who turned out to be a very good listener when she was getting paid.

All this listening gave Kathi the idea to become a psychiatrist. "Not a psychologist," she liked to stress. "I want to be able to write prescriptions."

Never one to start out humbly, my mother enrolled as a part-time student at the Harvard University Extension School. It was and still is an amazing program that offers Harvard curriculum and faculty to working adults at night. There is no admissions process, no SATs or letters of recommendation. Anyone who's able to pay the tuition can enroll, but to pass and earn credits is just as rigorous as you'd expect from a place like Harvard. My mother worked incredibly hard during her first few semesters, and became the proudest woman in Cambridge ever to pull a C.

The WASPy old women at the salon were tickled pink by their manicurist's aspirations. They invited my mother to their mansions and served her lunch. These women taught Kathi things like how to hold a knife and fork properly, and she would come home and pass this knowledge on to me. My mother talked excitedly about all her homework assignments—long readings by B. F. Skinner and Betty Friedan—while her clients regaled her with stories about their husbands' business trips in Europe, their vacation homes in Martha's Vineyard, their children away at boarding school.

"Boarding school?" Kathi's ears pricked up. "Now tell me, how do those work, exactly?"

Apparently, Mum explained to me later, these schools were all over New England and were full of the kinds of elitists she and I aspired to be. We went to the Danvers library and looked at some brochures. Next to glossy pictures of attractive, multicultural teenagers were bullet-point lists of the schools' offerings: a dozen foreign languages, every sport ever invented, art studios equipped with a dark room and a kiln. My mother and I skimmed over these details; as we did on all of our shopping excursions, we fixated on the price tag. The more expensive something was, the more we felt we needed it, and to run alongside those self-possessed teenagers for one year would cost the same as a brand-new car, a brand-new *European* car, something no one in the history of my family had ever owned.

Kathi rifled all the brochures into her purse. "They'll give you a scholarship," she said.

That year my mother and I took a tour of the ten most expensive boarding schools in New England. Every single one of these visits either began or ended in tears. On the morning of my interview, my mother would straighten my hair and, squirming just as much as I did when I was little, I'd end up getting burned with the flat iron. We were clueless about how we ought to appear, so Mum dressed me up like a prep-school fetish out of *Playboy* magazine. I wore the same costume to all my interviews—a short, pleated plaid skirt with a decorative safety pin and a mustard-yellow sweater set that was uncomfortably tight. When I argued for another outfit, Kathi blew a fuse and hurled the contents of our kitchen cabinets at my bedroom door.

"Would it kill you to show a little leg?" she groaned.

We'd drive to Exeter or Milton, my eyes still puffy and red from crying, and my mother would try to pump me full of confidence. "Tell them you're the smartest kid in your class and how much you love to learn. Don't be afraid to brag. They're impressed by kids who brag. You have to really sell yourself, Nik."

During the tours, my mother asked a million questions and addressed our student tour guides as "Honey." I skulked behind her, my eyes fixed on the ground. I didn't want to let myself fall in love with these schools. What would happen to me when I didn't get in?

Kathi hated to see me slouch. Once she stopped in the middle of a perfectly landscaped quad and started screaming, "What's wrong with you, Nikki? These kids are *smaht*. This is where you belong. Ask someone for their phone number." She spotted a teenager toting a cello case on his back. "*Honey*," she yelled to him. "Can my daughter call you and ask some questions about your academy? This is her right here. She's shy."

And so it was decided. I would go to public school for one year in the neighboring town of Hamilton, where there was a better than average academic program and a lottery for admitting a few students from other towns. I would use this time to pad my résumé while I applied to boarding schools.

Not more than ten minutes away from the town of Danvers, Hamilton was a different world. There is a country club called Myopia—a piece of found poetry that no one in the town seems to appreciate—where the queen of England once participated in a fox hunt. There are plenty of alcoholics there, but they don't show it on their faces the way people in Danvers do. Hamiltonians wear sweaters, not sweatshirts, and houses are on a septic system. Snob zoning, I would learn it was called. Communities on a septic system require bigger lots of land per house, therefore generating higher tax revenues. The reality of this—that pumping a household's shit into a tank buried in the backyard allowed for better public schools—was utterly revolting to me. My year at Hamilton High School became a painfully advanced lesson in American class warfare.

The truly wealthy in Hamilton sent their children off to the very private schools I was hoping would award me a scholarship, leaving the public high school full of upper-middle-class kids whose parents needed to save for college. With the super-rich culled from their ranks, the kids in Hamilton were dying for someone to outclass. I was a walking target. A week before my first day of high school, my mother had taken me on a manic shopping spree to the outlet stores in southern Maine. I had been wearing a plaid jumper for the past eight years and had no idea how to dress myself. I put all my trust in Kathi, who bought me hundred-dollar jeans that were so tight I couldn't cross my legs and logo-branded shirts that couldn't be sold at standard stores because they were "irregular."

These clothes advertised me as both an impostor and someone who was trying too hard to fit in, the two worst crimes you can commit in high school. I used a very scientific method in my efforts to deconstruct my fashion mistakes. Wool socks could be worn with Birkenstocks, but only with flared leg jeans; dyeing your hair magenta was a good move regardless of your skin tone, but bleach blondes were tacky unless they pierced their faces in at least three places, as this transformed peroxide into anti-aesthetic rebellion. As trenchant as these observations were, I could never figure out how to pull a functional outfit together. Like natural flexibility or singing in key, it's a skill some people are just born with.

Hamilton is the kind of lily-white New England town where Jews, Italians, and Greeks are considered exotic, and even those tiny distinctions melted away as long as you spoke with the right diction. Every time I opened my mouth to speak, the kids in my classes would snicker and exchange looks. I wasn't aware that I had an accent until then.

"Say *car* again," my classmates taunted. "Say *hair*."

Naïvely, I'd repeat the words they told me to say, and they'd laugh in my face.

The New England accent, unlike the southern one, is not considered cute or sexy. No one has ever been called charming when she added a nasal extra syllable to the preposition *for*. There are subtle variations in diction from state to state that only an insider can detect. I wince when movie actors playing Bostonians sound like rural Mainers, just as I've known Kentuckians to explode when it's assumed, as many casting directors do, that everyone with a twang is from Georgia. From what I've observed, though, while complicated and nuanced—and, I'm sure, delightful to tourists and linguistics PhDs alike—southern accents extend across class lines, whereas the New England accent does not. Dropping your *r*'s means one thing only: you are ignorant, broke-ass, uncultured trash. A handful of extremely handsome white boys can get away with saying they drink at "bahs in Hahvid," and only in their twenties. These same words coming from a woman or an overweight man, or anyone over thirty, will inspire looks of pity and derision.

Although I failed to master the dress code of the preppy, hippie, or punk-rock kids at Hamilton High (those were the only three alternatives), I did discover a gift for language and imitation. I spent the first few months of ninth grade listening to the way the kids at Hamilton talked, training myself à la Eliza Doolittle, until I had a nice, innocuous inflection completely devoid of regional color. Like many people who have crossed over an imaginary line to pursue higher education, I have since lost my ability even to fake a Boston accent. Only in primitive emotional states, when I'm screaming at someone I love, or saying the Lord's Prayer, does a vestige of my old voice bleat through.

"Ah Fathah, Who aht in heaven . . ."

By the time I had this figured out, it was too late for me at Hamilton High. Everyone knew exactly who I was—a girl from another town, a town where we pumped our sewage out to a plant and where people swallowed the letter *r*.

The only person willing to associate with me was another out-of-towner named Julie, whose accent was slighter than mine (both her parents had graduated from college) but was still noticeable enough to get her branded. Julie and I forged a bond over the mutually accepted lie that we were going to become new people in this new school. After months of eating my lunch alone in the girls' bathroom (the one next to the gym, because it got the least traffic), I finally had someone saving a seat for me in the cafeteria. With her curly hair and her loud infectious laugh, Julie eventually recruited enough other girls to fill a small table. These were nice Hamiltonian kids with limp ponytails and porcelain skin, living portraits of virginity. One of them was Katie, a tall and freakishly thin girl with bony elbow joints always bent at acute angles. The daughter of two teachers, Katie and her family had just moved to Hamilton so that she could get into the school system without entering the lottery. She was nerdy and smart and had an endless fount of self-esteem that astounded me. I loved doing my homework at her big, clean house after school. Her refrigerator was filled with exotic yuppie foods I'd never heard of, like hummus and smoked salmon. Her parents subscribed to *The New Yorker* and didn't mind at all when I asked if I could take home their old issues. I'd been collecting the magazine's covers from doctors' offices since I was a kid and had papered an entire wall of my bedroom with them.

Right away my mother smelled trouble. "Don't let those people fool you," she warned me before dropping me off at Katie's house. "They're just teachers."

After hanging out at Katie's for a few weeks, I invited her to sleep over at my house one Friday night. I don't know what I was thinking— proof of my place somewhere on the autism spectrum, or another undiagnosable deficiency in self-awareness. How else could I have believed that this sleepover would go well?

As long as I live, I will never forget the look on Katie's face as my mother drove us down Eden Glen Avenue and parked in front of our house. Katie touched the little gold charm on her necklace the way the nuns sometimes clutched their rosary beads, with horror and fear.

"Ohmygod!" she exclaimed. "Your house is so—cute!"

Our roof was festooned with drooping Christmas lights hung and then forgotten so many years ago that all the color had peeled off the bulbs. The porch was loaded with bags of trash next to but not inside the trash cans, and our front door was frosted with bird shit. (My mother refused to evict the purple martins that nested on our porch.) There was even an old toilet on the porch. It was the toilet of my mother's childhood, long broken and removed from the bathroom but never taken the extra twelve paces to the curb for trash day. Mum and I used to joke about planting flowers inside the bowl, and maybe some basil in the tank. I tried to explain this to Katie. Surely she would get the sardonic wit of it all.

Katie held her overnight bag close to her chest as she climbed the steps of our front porch. The cheap wallpaper we had put up to cover the wood paneling was already peeling off in golden, smoke-stained curls. More beer cans and trash bags of junk were piled inside the kitchen and in the hallway to my room, crowding the floor space. My mother went shopping in the same fury she consumed her drugs. During her sober spells, she filled the void in her life with rabid consumerism. I don't even know what she bought, just . . . *stuff.* Packages of new bedsheets she would lose in the mess and later have to replace. Packages of exotic spices she would lose inside the kitchen cabinets. Thigh-high leather boots she would never wear. Cans of metallic paint for that make-believe day when we finally renovated our house. It was the pursuit and never the bounty that thrilled her. Swiping her credit card at the register of even the lowliest bargain basement, basking in that singular capitalist illusion of purchasable control—this was for her the climax of the shopping experience. Once home, whatever she'd bought was immediately forgotten and added to the wayside of her neglect.

It was a lot to keep up with in our little house, especially considering that both she and Michael found it hard to part with anything, even legitimate trash. When an ashtray filled up, which could happen in a span of a few hours, my stepfather would reach for the nearest coffee cup or Styrofoam take-out container and fill that rather than empty the ashtray. The two of them saved issues of *TV Guide* the way other people saved *National Geographic*. Which is to say, they let them pile up on the floor with everything else.

I was used to living like this and had made my bedroom a temple of spartan, minimalist order. On my mantel, spaced precisely three inches apart, I had what I described then as "artsy" pictures culled from magazines: a pair of red high heels casting a long Expressionistic shadow; a wolf looking solemnly into a distant field; a tiny reprint of van Gogh's *Starry Night*. I matted these pictures on squares of cardboard that I attacked with glitter and glue. My bed was made with hospital corners, and the night before Katie came over I had vacuumed and dusted from floor to ceiling. I didn't do all this for her alone, though I hoped Katie would notice my good housekeeping. Thursday vacuuming was a ritual for me, and if I tried to leave my bedroom without arranging my pillows *just so*, I would get a burning pain in my stomach and have to go back to remake it.

The door to my bedroom had two holes kicked in the bottom and the footprints of my mother's size-seven shoe. Katie had tact enough not to ask about the holes, but I think they scared her, because she refused to venture beyond my room alone and made me escort her to and from the bathroom. The next morning, her mother came to pick her up and Katie never called me again. She was friendly to me at school, but there were no more sleepovers or homework dates or invitations to the movies.

At Catholic school there had been lots of onetime sleepovers and girls who were allowed to invite me over to their house but couldn't spend time at mine. I had always ascribed that to my unwed mother and the moral threat she posed. We stank of sin, not trash. Katie was suggesting something altogether different. Here was a smart girl from a progressive-minded family. They read the *New York Times* and begged for the freedom of all sorts of political martyrs via bumper stickers on their minivan. If someone like Katie couldn't sympathize with me, who in the world ever would?

It didn't matter, I told myself. I would be leaving Katie and the rest of them behind for boarding school soon enough.

When springtime came, the rejection letters filled our mailbox. I was furious at my mother. I blamed her completely, not for my failures but for making me believe that I had a chance in the first place.

"See!" I shouted at her. "Only *you* think I'm smart. No one else does! Big fish in a small pond. Nothing more! Do you get it now?" I slammed my door, threw myself on my bed, and sobbed.

"We still haven't heard from Phillips Academy," Mum said from the hallway. Her voice was calm and reassuring, and this made me want to strangle her so badly that my hands shook.

"Andover is, like, the hardest school I applied to. Are you really that delusional? There's no way in hell . . ."

The letter we were waiting for finally arrived. Phillips Academy Andover had accepted me as a new tenth grader that fall. A year's tuition plus room and board there cost more than most state colleges, but they sent along another letter saying they had some money set aside just for me. Not a "full boat ride," as we say in New England, but ninety percent of a boat ride.

I learned all this from my mother, whom I called every day from the pay phone in the lobby of the high school. Katie was standing there with me, along with Julie and a gaggle of wide-eyed virgins. When I hung up the phone, I started to cry. I had won the lottery. I was leaving!

"Oh my God, congratulations." Katie forced herself to smile. I saw her brow wrinkle as she tried to assimilate this news into her worldview. What did this say about her and me and the differences between us? The little cogs inside her brain were slowly turning. I could almost smell the smoke. Soon she had her answer.

"If you ever get date-raped at boarding school, you *have* to call me. I will totally be your counselor," she said.

THE DAY BEFORE I moved to Andover was the hottest day of the summer. My mother and I walked warily around each other like two pieces of flint that might catch fire if we touched. I had a long list of things to do—laundry and last-minute shopping, in addition to cleaning my mother's house one last time. No one else would so much as throw away an empty pack of cigarettes while I was gone, so I wanted to be thorough. I was so anxious that it was hard to focus on anything. I remember dropping and breaking several dishes that day. My mother gave me a glass of water to hold while she searched for a hairbrush in her purse, and I spilled it all over a pile of papers, letters to the new parent of an Andover student that she had been avoiding all summer.

"I can't stand you when you're like this!" My mother slammed her fist on the kitchen table. "I can't stand it!"

All day long we screamed and fought about everything except the real thing between us: I was leaving. My mother was envious, heartbroken, and scared, but, more than that, more than anything, she was proud.

MY ROOM WAS ON the top floor of a dorm called Paul Revere Hall. I'd picked out a black-and-white-striped comforter for my bed and decorated the walls with black-and-white posters of Martin Luther King, Jr., and U2. There was nothing with color in my room except an iridescent beta fish named Figaro who lived in a tiny glass bowl on my dresser. All the girls in my dorm that year had the same hunter-green floral-print bedspread from a designer I'd never heard of named Laura Ashley. I'm not exaggerating when I say everyone. For a second, both Kathi and I wondered if it had been issued by the school and mine had been lost in the mail.

Of all the girls in that esteemed academy, the one to be randomly assigned as my roommate was none other than the great-great-granddaughter of Emily Post, doyenne of American etiquette. I was sure that this girl would judge me as a freak raised by wolves, but Anna Post turned out to be a practical, kindhearted roommate whose parents had taught her to rise above petty snobbery.

Anna Post was the first of many people I would meet whose last name signified something more than where one was seated in homeroom. (Besides, we didn't have homerooms at Andover.) After we had unpacked, my mother and I pored over the directory of students, where everyone's picture and home address were listed. We scanned the pages in search of the rich and famous. My classmates at Andover were the sons and daughters of senators, governors, and foreign heads of state whose names were so renowned that even my mother and I easily recognized them. There were other kids whose last names were printed on the labels of products we had in our kitchen, bathroom, and garage.

Kathi began hunting for my future husband. "What about So-and-So?" she asked me after discovering a boy in my grade who was from the family that manufactured the number-one-selling dishwashing detergent in the nation.

I took the directory from her. "He looks like a frog," I said.

"Who cares? There are a lot more important things than looks. Honey, when you grow up, you'll learn how easy it is to just shut your eyes, hold your breath, and fuck someone." She studied this particular boy's face and frowned. "But you're right," she conceded. "There's nothing uglier than an ugly WASP. Poor little thing."

MY FIRST NIGHT IN the dorm was hard, not because I was away from home and my family but because we weren't allowed to have televisions in our rooms and, except for camping trips, I had never fallen asleep without one flickering softly in the background. For the first time in my life, I lay alone in the true silence of nighttime. My heart was beating so fast that I considered calling an ambulance. I covered my face with a pillow and swallowed the urge to cry. In the next room, I heard the sound of Anna weeping in her bed. If *she* couldn't handle being here, I was sure I never would. I started to cry, then immediately blacked out as though struck in the head with the blunt force of all my emotions at once. When I opened my eyes again, it was morning. *This is my new home, I have to make this work,* I repeated a hundred times a day like a prayer. If I failed at Andover, I told myself, I would not live to be eighteen.

My dorm was full of bright, interesting girls from around the world. Class difference didn't matter to them nearly as much as to the kids at my public school, because these girls slept on mattresses stuffed with ostrich feathers and hundred-dollar bills and wore pajamas that were more expensive than my prom dress would be. They had enough money not to harbor any class anxiety. We were all so eager to re-create a semblance of family life in the dorm that the things we would ordinarily hide from our friends, at least at first, came tumbling out early on. Late one night during that first week of school, I confessed to my roommate that I had been conceived and born out of wedlock. Her response had more class and grace than any other I've heard.

"You were a *love child*!" Anna said. "That's *sooo* romantic!"

She assured me that a genesis like mine was essential to becoming the heroine of an epic life story. I liked Anna's brand of grandiosity a lot more than my mother's. When the kids at Catholic school or their parents said something snide about my illegitimacy, Kathi would say, "What the fuck? Chrissie Hynde had Ray Davies's baby, and that all turned out fine."

Around most everyone outside my dorm, I was so afraid of saying the wrong thing that I refused to say anything at all. I ate my meals as quickly and inconspicuously as possible in the Andover Commons, an odd name, I thought, for a dining hall with glittering nineteenth-century chandeliers. For weeks I would run back to my room after dinner and call my mother in tears.

"Why aren't you making friends?" Mum asked me. "Maybe you smell bad, Honey. Do you wear deodorant?"

"Yes."

"Every day?"

"Of course!"

"Put on some lipstick. You don't even try to look pretty, do you?"

There were Saturday classes every other weekend, which felt like a godsend. It meant two Friday nights a month when I didn't have to lie about why I didn't have social plans. I usually spent weekends listening to the same Radiohead CD over and over on my cheap boom box. Every single weekend that we were allowed to leave campus, I went home.

"Those girls are all jealous of you," my mother said, trying to console me. Kathi couldn't seem to make up her mind: one minute I was too hideous to appear in public without bringing deep shame on the family; a second later, my beauty was so staggering that it alienated commoners on the street.

"The other girls in your dorm can't stand you because you're so gorgeous. You should see the way they look at you. They want to kill you. But you're lucky. You have me. Mummy will always be your friend. I'm your best friend."

And she was. For that one year, we were finally on the same level: I turned fifteen, and Mum, in her better moods, had the emotional maturity of a fifteen-year-old. I was at Andover, and she was plugging away at her Harvard Extension bachelor's degree one credit at a time. We both stressed over our homework and found relief in the same movies and music.

The girls in my dorm were always having spontaneous dance parties in their rooms. I would hear them laughing and jumping around on the other side of the wall. All I had to do was knock on their door and I would be welcomed inside, but it was impossible for me to do this. Back home, my mother and I blasted her stereo with the same songs the girls at school were listening to, Blondie and the Talking Heads and New Order. We turned it up loud enough to make the windows rattle, but we never, ever danced.

It was a funny inhibition, considering that Kathi was utterly lacking in social restraint. There is a ripple of meat in the frontal lobe responsible for impulse control. When the neurons are firing appropriately, it prevents most of us from, let's say, telling the hostess of a crowded restaurant to go fuck herself because we're hungry and all the tables happen to be full. This part of my mother's brain was a blitzkrieg. Her emotions could erupt anywhere, at any time—at a department store, in a dentist's office, on an airplane. If I tried to intervene, all the radiation she was leaking would concentrate into one furious laser beam aimed right at me. I'd learned the hard way that the only thing I could do in these moments was step back and watch her detonate.

Whenever she visited my dorm, my mother would walk around deliberately making a mess of my fastidiously clean room. "Uh-oh!" she'd say as she upset a stack of papers on my desk. Turning my hairbrush a few degrees so that it no longer lay parallel with the edge of the dresser, she'd look me in the eye and say, "Oh, sorry, Hon. Is this bothering you?" She'd pull a book out one inch from its neighbors on a shelf, laugh herself silly, then sit on my bed and light a cigarette.

"Mum, please don't," I begged. "We're not allowed." I opened a window and fanned the smoke away from the smoke detector.

"Relax. They can't do anything to me. I'm a parent."

And yet the simple, instinctual impulse to dance alone in one's bedroom had this brazen bear of a woman shrinking inside herself, and, like a still helpless extension of my mother's body, I shrank, too. I could tell by the way she nodded to the music and swayed, just a little, that inside my mother there was a woman—a girl, really—roiling with dammed-up movement.

I EVENTUALLY MADE FRIENDS with two girls in my dorm, falling in love in that consuming, half-homoerotic way young girls do. For about three weeks, Maggie, Cecily, and I ate every meal together. We'd camp out in my room at night, staying up until dawn, giggling and doing our homework. We would laugh until we fell asleep, the three of us squished into a tiny twin bed like kittens, only to wake up the next morning still laughing. On the third weekend of our friendship I went home, and while I was gone these two friends bonded over some arbitrarily evil pact to shun me.

"Cecily can't stand the way you eat," Maggie whispered to me in the bathroom the Sunday night I returned. "You hunch over your tray like someone's going to steal it from you. It's embarrassing." She ran her fingers nervously through her hair. It was a different color, I noticed, a coppery red. She and Cecily must have dyed it that weekend. "She told me to just ignore you when you got back to the dorm, like, don't even talk to you at all. Don't explain. But that seemed mean. So . . ."

This kind of thing happened every weekend, if not to me then to someone else. A girls' dorm is full of all the vicious drama but little of the pornography one assumes. I'm sure some girls were having sex with each other, but I was out of the loop. It was overwhelming enough for me just to have friends. We chastely seduced, ensnared, dumped, tortured, forgave, fawned over, petted, rivaled, envied, disgraced, despised, and nurtured one another, and I loved and dreaded every minute of it.

Despite the savagery of girls during these seminal years, or maybe because of it, I think there is no better place for a teenager's development than a boarding-school dormitory. In playing our little mind games, we were performing a critical exercise—sharpening ourselves like swords for what lay ahead. At a certain point it became clear that there were things that belonged to us, and things that were only for boys. We held exclusive rights to field hockey, eating disorders, Parliament cigarettes, menstrual periods, accessorizing, and tears. The boys had dominion over skateboards, snowboards, Marlboros, jerking off, open showers, and violence. Some things were anathema regardless of gender, like popping zits or missing your family—you did them only in private and prayed that no one caught you in the act. Certain things we agreed to share in the same way we claimed or rejected everything else, tacitly and with complete consensus. The Beastie Boys and Ritalin had the ability to cross camps, as did falling in love, getting dumped, wanting to fuck, and wanting to kill yourself.

The movie *Pulp Fiction* should have been subsumed into the boys-only category, but the girls of Paul Revere got hold of it first. There was a lot of hype about this movie when it was released. The violence was supposedly graphic and disturbing, so much so that movie theaters across the country cracked down on checking IDs before you entered the theater, meaning that only a couple of kids from New

York City had actually seen it. The house counselors at Paul Revere were pretty supportive of any weekend activity that didn't leave us pregnant or dead, so not only did they rent *Pulp Fiction* for us one Saturday night, they baked us cookies, too.

The entire dorm showed up to watch the movie on the common-room TV. The field-hockey Sarahs and Meghans, Connecticut blondes with doe eyes and patrician noses; the impeccably dressed Hong Kong girls, Alice and Angie; June and Margaret, the two black girls from the Bronx, a place I found no less exotic than Hong Kong; Heather, the white girl from Saudi Arabia by way of Texas; Sana, the Muslim girl from Saudi Arabia by way of Sri Lanka; Shiva, the skinny, witty Indian girl from western Massachusetts; Anna, my roommate from Vermont; Maggie and Cecily, my on-again, off-again best friends; and me. As many girls as possible squeezed together on two itchy couches. The rest of us sprawled out on the floor, lying on one another's laps, leaning on shoulders, braiding and unbraiding one another's hair.

We had everything and nothing in common. The entire student body of Andover was smart, hardworking, and ambitious, but what I loved most about my dorm mates was that they imploded my entire paradigm of intelligence. I had always been quick to pick up foreign languages and could easily parse the symbolism of an epic poem, but the girls in Paul Revere were good at everything—chemistry, physics, and differential calculus. And they weren't just clever; they were aware. I saw this so clearly that night as a coolly violent movie lit up our faces. One scene in particular nearly started a riot in the basement of our dorm. Bruce Willis's character is getting ready for his big escape on a dead man's motorcycle and his girlfriend, played by Maria de Medeiros, is stalling him with all her womanish questions.

"That girl talks like a baby," some Meghan or Sarah said with disgust. "She's so fucking stupid."

"Why does she have to be so stupid?" someone else asked.

"Because she's a *girl,* Stupid."

We all cracked up laughing.

"Shh!"

"God, I can't stand how stupid this French chick is. Her voice. Ugh."

"She's like a child."

"That's why guys think she's hot, you know."

"So gross."

"Do you know what my mother said to me on the phone tonight? She said that I have too much testosterone. Seriously. She thinks I have a chemical imbalance and need medication because I'm 'too aggressive.' Can you believe that?"

"What a bitch."

"*Shhhhh!*"

"Shut up!"

It wasn't until I met these girls that I finally started to think for myself and make decisions about who I wanted to be, even if these decisions were silent and subterranean still. The girls at Andover were the first people in my life to teach me how to grow up.

AND YET MY MOTHER insisted that I was a late bloomer. She couldn't mean boobs, because I had those in sixth grade, or intellectual maturity, because I was a decade ahead of her by the time I left high school, which she was the first to admit. No, Kathi was referring to her daughter's latent interest in drugs.

"Nikki's totally square," Mum used to tell her non-sober friends, as though apologizing for me.

Once, while we were on vacation in Cape Cod, my mother picked up a hitchhiker, a harmless college boy who was too drunk to walk home. He sat in the front seat and lit up a joint, which he offered to everyone in the car, including my ten-year-old cousin, Fafa, and me. I tried to say no in as cool a way as possible. The hitchhiker was cute in a crunchy, hippie sort of way, and I wanted him to read a complicated subtext in my refusal, like maybe I was an Olympic hopeful in figure skating and subject to random drug tests. Or, at the tender age of twelve, I had already smoked both pot and crack, but not anymore—I was on the wagon these days.

"Nikki's too ambitious to smoke grass," my mother said to the kid sitting next to her. "Look at her." She turned around and laughed. "Right now she's wondering if this moment is going to come up in her Senate hearing when she gets nominated for the Supreme Court."

It was partly true. At twelve I hadn't ruled out a career in politics. But at that moment in time my only aspiration was for my mother's car to drive off a bridge and drown us all so that I wouldn't have to hear the sound of her and the hitchhiker laughing at me.

It was not until the summer after my first year at Andover that I started smoking pot. I'd maintained a friendship with Julie from Hamilton High, and we smoked for the first time at her family's summer camp in New Hampshire. Julie informed me that it was a medical fact you couldn't get high the first time you smoked but that I might as well get the first time over with so that the next time would be better. I'd really like to know who started this rumor, because the first time I smoked pot I felt like my face was going to slide off my head.

Teenagers are bigger children who are embarrassed by how much they still want to run around and just *play*. That's when and why hallucinogens walk onstage. Smoking pot or eating mushrooms turned everyday objects into toys. It gave us permission to be imaginative and silly. As Julie and I finished that first joint, a family of ducks swam by in a row, all of them bobbing for fish, and I laughed with an ease and a shamelessness that I hadn't felt since I was a little kid.

When I got home and told my mother what I'd done, she got on the phone and called the sisters she was still speaking to. "You'll never believe it!" she said, beaming. "Nikki got high!"

From then on my mother made sure to stuff a nickel bag of pot, always green, sticky, and fragrant, into my stocking at Christmas. She didn't smoke pot herself. For her it was a preadolescent experiment; by the time she was a freshman in high school, she had permanently moved on to hard drugs. Mum remembered fondly the pleasure potheads found in salty and sweet snack foods, so once I started getting high she made sure the cabinets were stocked with good "munchables." If I was getting high with a boyfriend, she might even cook for us.

Kathi was my first drug dealer, and without a doubt the best one I ever had. She never ripped me off, in fact, she never charged me, and she always had access to higher quality stuff than the ponytailed high-school dropouts my friends bought from. My mother's big claim to fame was that she once sold cocaine to Steven Tyler, of Aerosmith. This was before MTV and the big-arena shows, back when Aerosmith was still a local Boston band. I don't know anything else about it, except that one sentence my mother repeated when she was feeling insignificant or dejected—*"I sold coke to Steven Tyler, you know"*—each word a sharp note until the last, released with a sigh and a puff of smoke.

My mother didn't fuss over me as much once I started smoking pot. She seemed relieved. I had friends coming over to the house when I was home and another set of girls to hang out with at school. I moved seamlessly, though not without guilt and tiny pricks of shame, between my two different worlds. This is fairly typical of scholarship kids at prep schools. My Andover friendships felt more like business associates. Finishing our homework and getting high without getting caught were occupations we shared. We studied together, baked cupcakes in the dorm counselor's apartment, debated about Kant and free will versus determinism, practiced our Russian with elderly immigrants, tutored inner-city children after school, and found every possible opportunity to sneak into the woods and get stoned. Back home I became known as the girl who lived in That House, the broken-down one with no rules. Kids from my old public high school and then friends of their friends discovered that they could drink and smoke at my place with impunity. There were times when I would return home from boarding school to find kids I had never met before sitting on my porch, smoking cigarettes. They would nod at me sullenly, as if to say, "What are *you* doing here?"

I was well into my twenties before I realized that the people you sit next to while ripping bong hits or blowing lines off a CD case weren't the same as friends. Drug friendships are shaky alliances. Kids would steal pills from my mother while I was away at school, and then snort them without me. Those were *my* pills to steal, not theirs. Lucky for them, the price of my mercy was cheap. Back then, an offering of high-grade pot or a case of Budweiser was all it took to forgive and forget.

35 Eden Glen Avenue became a haven for the stoned and the wasted. My mother wanted it that way. She thought it was safer, and I guess it was. No one I knew ever careened off a highway or wrapped his car around a telephone pole. Violent hangovers were the most dramatic consequences any of us faced, and I was usually the one kneeling over the toilet. I was allowed to do whatever I wanted, go wherever I felt like going at any time of the day or night, as long as I called my mother and reported in to her every couple of hours.

"Hey, Mum, we're going to eat mushrooms at Singing Beach and then crash at Kevin's place. His parents are out of town."

"Okay, Honey. Call me later to check in. Wait a minute—who's driving?"

"Jesse."

"I don't like the way that Jesse drives. Tell him I said to slow down or I'll kill him myself."

If I forgot to check in with my mother, all hell would break loose. One spring break a group of college friends and I drove down to New Orleans. This was in the days before cell phones, so I had to stop every couple of hundred miles to call my mother from a highway pay phone. After a few days on the road and several dozen joints, we arrived at our youth hostel ready to eat our way through the city. The hostel manager recommended a nearby restaurant, so we went there first and ordered gumbo. Feeling confident, I tacked a beer on to my order, coolly, casually, as if it was an afterthought. "Bud Light in the bottle. If you have it," I added, so that she wouldn't think it was a big deal. The waitress didn't ask for an ID, and I sat there sweating until she returned and plopped the beer down without incident.

"I'm serious, you guys. I'm moving here," I told my friends. "New Orleans is the only enlightened city in the U.S."

We ate and drank and smoked and listened to live music. The night was young, and we were planning our next move when the waitress came over to our table and stared at me.

"Um, is your name Domenica?" she asked.

My heart stopped. "Why?"

"Your mother's looking for you. She's on the phone right now."

Horrified, I got up from the table.

"Phone's behind the bar," the waitress said, then, behind my back, I heard her tell my friends, "That woman is scary."

"Oh my God, Mum?"

"You forgot to call me," my mother sang in a creepy voice.

When she hadn't heard from me, Kathi had called her credit-card company to find out where I had checked in, then called the hostel and spoke to the manager to see if he knew where I had gone.

"But how did the waitress know who I was?" I asked her.

"Oh, that was the easy part." My mother laughed. "I just told her to look for a teenage girl with ratty brown hair and black eyebrows. 'If she's a foot and a half shorter than all her friends, that's my daughter.' "

"I'm so sorry. I'm so, so—"

"It's okay, Honey. I just wanted to make sure you were still alive. Be careful, okay? Mummy would have to kill herself if anything ever happened to you. You know that."

"I'm so sorry."

"Have a good time. Call me tomorrow!"

I never forgot to call her again.

SOMETIME DURING MY SENIOR year at Andover, my mother told me not to come home for the next few weekends. Why? I asked her. She had started shooting heroin again and was trying to get herself off it.

"I'm going to be really sick, Hon. I don't want to scare you. I don't want you to see me this way."

Kathi didn't stay up all night talking anymore, as she did when she was on coke. There were several bottles of pills at her bedside, but that was nothing new. I knew that she had dropped out of her classes at the Harvard Extension School and that she had quit her job at the salon, but heroin? How could I have missed something like that? Probably because I was so stoned myself.

For as long as I was a conscious being, my mother had been afflicted with some incurable pain. First she was recovering from a car accident. A few years later, when she was thirty-four, she had a hysterectomy. This surgery, I'm certain, was unnecessary, a solution concocted by a male doctor trying to shut up what he generalized as another complaining woman. The hysterectomy caused a slew of reactions, one disease after another. These diseases were elusive and always changing. Some of them were very real—my mother had lost her uterus and both ovaries in one scoop; it was only natural that her body would howl in protest. But some illnesses were most definitely her invention, a ploy to get prescriptions for stronger pills.

At some point in my adolescence, the brief period of sobriety ended and my mother's pills became bigger and stronger. She was always good about sharing—with my stepfather, with her so-called friends, with my own so-called friends. Even her dog, an obese Dalmatian that was dying of cancer, got licks from the plate she used to crush up and snort her pills. Naturally, she shared her pills with her own daughter, too.

The first time I took one of my mother's pills I was ten years old. I had a headache and we didn't have any aspirin. We never had any practical stuff like that in our house. I doubt we had Band-Aids or Q-tips that day, either. But we were well stocked with Percocet and Vicodin and Ativan. Whenever I went to a friend's house and complained of a headache, I would look at the aspirin I was given with confusion. "Is this really all you have?" I felt like saying. I assumed that other people's mothers were just stingy.

Then came a new pill, OxyContin. My mother had lots of pet names for her pills. I wish I could remember all of them—Oscar de la Rentas, Oscar De La Hoyas, and, in honor of the Academy Awards, plain old Oscars. It was a prescription painkiller new to the market in the 1990s. On the off chance that you haven't heard of it, here is a little analogy:

OXYCONTIN : HEROIN :: MARGARINE : BUTTER

These two drugs follow the same pathway through the human body, producing the same chain of reactions from bloodstream to brain, except that one is derived from natural opiates harvested in an Afghan poppy field and the other is synthetically engineered by the Purdue Pharma corporation. My mother had a rotation of specialists whom she consulted for her various ailments, and all of these doctors were men who doled out OxyContin as though the pharmaceutical companies were giving complimentary blow jobs for every new prescription they wrote. In 2001, OxyContin was the highest legally sold drug of its kind. And it was all over the street. Kathi was one of the first people in our area to get a prescription.

I'll never forget the day she broke a twenty-milligram Oscar in half, giving me one piece to swallow as she snorted the other half in solidarity. I don't remember why she did this. I might have complained about a headache. Maybe I was crying over a fight I'd had with one of my toxic, ephemeral best friends. Mum never distinguished between physical and emotional pain, especially when she had a pill that could cure both.

Imagine a hundred-pound teenager on the equivalent of one bump of heroin. The moment the pill kicked in, there was a warmth in my stomach that spread to my arms and legs. I could feel my heart pulsing in my hands, and every beat seemed to pump a new surge of contentment and hope into my veins. I floated from my bedroom down the hall to the bathroom, where I knelt on the filthy tiled floor and vomited a day's worth of food in less than thirty seconds. Puking violently, I swear I have never felt so good in my entire life. I had an overwhelming urge to tell my mother how much I loved her, but there I was, hugging the toilet bowl for Act 2 of my own private opera.

When I was finally through, I rinsed my mouth and climbed up onto Kathi's bed.

"Mum," I said as I lay down beside her, "you are my best friend in the whole world."

"I know I am, Honey." She raked her long fingernails through my hair, something she hadn't done since I was a little girl. "I always will be."

Mang

M Y MOTHER ONCE HAD A DRUG DEALER WHO FELL MADLY IN
love with her. His name was Oliver. He had a football player's build,
shaved his head to the bone every morning, lived in the city of Lynn,
a notoriously crime-ridden satellite of Boston, and was briefly a
member of the Nation of Islam.

Or, as Mum put it in her first descriptive sentence of him, "Ol's
black!"

Oliver lent Kathi a stack of his favorite CDs, which she listened to
like an obsessive teenager. "Ol likes that rap music," she told me.
"It's not usually my thing, but have you heard of the rapper Notorious B.I.G.? He's really good. He reminds me of me."

I had just finished my first semester of college, where Biggie's
album *Life After Death* was a staple in my dorm. It was late December of 1997. I scribbled the answers to my last final exam as fast as I
could and caught a direct flight back to Boston. My heart had been
pounding the whole day with the fearful, euphoric rhythm that always carried me home. After landing, I waited for about three hours
at Logan Airport for my mother to pick me up, then got on a pay
phone to call her collect.

"Where are you?"

"Where are *you*?"

She had completely forgotten that I was coming home that day.

"I'm on my way right now, Honey. Oooh, I have so many surprises for you! Just you wait!"

One of them was the white Lincoln Navigator SUV she arrived in. It was a luxury war chariot that got about twelve miles to the gallon, the vehicle of choice for multiplatinum-selling pop stars that year. Mum didn't know any of this when she started leasing hers. She just picked out the biggest thing on the lot.

"Sometimes, when I'm stuck in traffic, I fantasize about driving right over the other cars," Mum told me. "I could really do it, you know. Did you see the size of those tires?"

Looking out the window, I realized how high we were elevated. "It feels like wearing platform shoes," I said.

"Oh, I almost forgot!" Mum cried, then reached across my lap to open the glove box. She pulled out a tiny stainless-steel revolver with mother-of-pearl inlay on the handle. "Look! It's white to match the 'Gator. Do you want one for Christmas?"

Her new friend Oliver had *connections,* she said. He promised to hook her up with another pistol for next to nothing. I politely declined.

"Are you crazy?" My mother waved her little gun in the air. "At that price, it would be a waste *not* to buy another one. Come on. We can take a class together so it'll be totally safe and legal. Get certified and everything."

I handled the gun with my scarf and returned it to the glove box. "Didn't you just say this gun was stolen?"

"Jesus, Nikki. Do you ever get exhausted being you?"

With the gun now out of sight, I relaxed and stretched my legs. Fiddling with the dials on the seat, I found that there was enough room for me to kick my feet in the air without grazing the dashboard. There was also a seat warmer. I helped myself to one of my mother's cigarettes and reclined way, way back. The Navigator made me very nervous (too big, too white, too expensive—I didn't see this ending well), but I had to admit it was a comfortable ride, and hard-core rap sounded so good booming through its speakers.

The sky that day was a soiled white sheet sagging with the threat of snow. We rounded a corner. Bright flashes of silver shivered then vanished through gaps in the trees. The ocean. I was home.

When we got to Eden Glen Avenue, Mum transferred Oliver's CD to the stereo. She'd recently bought a new sound system outfitted with eight small, state-of-the-art speakers that she piled up on the cardboard boxes they came in. This whole setup was worth more than every other electronic appliance in our house combined; it was probably more expensive than the negligible slice of tuition my college scholarship didn't cover, which my mother was reliably delinquent in paying. That stereo had a lot of weight to pull in a house that was otherwise in shambles. New floors, roof, plumbing, and heating were long overdue when we had moved in six years earlier. Now there were holes in the floor that glimmered light from the kitchen above when I did laundry in the cellar. It was no longer safe to drink water from the tap, and there was an infestation of both rats and squirrels that I could hear fighting inside the walls at night.

The most significant change during the past few months that I'd been away at college was the crack pipe on the coffee table. There had always been paraphernalia hidden around the house while I was growing up. Items would turn up from time to time like a sloppy Easter-egg hunt. Searching for a lost TV remote, I would open a curtain or lift a towel off a cardboard box and find a burned spoon and the cap of a disposable syringe. Now, it seemed, my parents were leaving it all out in the open as casually as they would a pair of dirty socks.

Kathi skipped ahead to her favorite track on Oliver's CD, "The Ten Crack Commandments." It's a violent, nihilistic yet danceable how-to guide for dealing crack cocaine. My mother knew every word by heart:

"Keep your fam'ly and business / completely separated / Money and blood don't mix / Like two dicks and one bitch / You find yourself in serious shit. . . ."

She turned up the volume as loud as it would go, then went outside to the porch and shot her two middle fingers at our neighbors' house. Her knees bobbed in a funny, fat-white-lady dance. I knew that I had grown up a great deal when I saw her do this, because for the first time I was not embarrassed by but *for* her.

I turned down the stereo. Mum came back inside and lit a cigarette. "I just love it when Ol comes and picks me up. The neighbors look at us in horror. I told him, 'Play your music loud enough to give all these fucks aneurysms, Ol!' He thinks I'm a riot."

It had been a long time since I'd seen my mother this happy. She started chopping garlic for a sauce that would eventually burn, so rapt was she in her quixotic tale of interracial love.

OLIVER WAS A SUCCESSFUL drug dealer on the North Shore and my mother was one of his best clients. He would drive up from Lynn to make his deliveries to her and afterward he and my mother would go for a ride. "He has the same Lincoln I do, same year and everything, only his is black!" Mum swooned. They would ride around for hours together, talking and enjoying the well-preserved scenery of Cape Ann, a tiny lobe of rock bulging just north of Boston. If they saw a nice house that was for sale, they'd stop and collect real-estate flyers. Oliver had lived in the city of Lynn all his life and he was sick of the robberies and the stabbings. He'd saved enough money over the years to move to the suburbs. My mother gave him the scoop on every single town in the area, recommending, above all, that he buy a house on the water. She had spent her entire life gazing at the same river from her kitchen window and couldn't imagine how anyone could get along otherwise.

"He tells me over and over that he's in love with me," Mum said. "And I'm, like, 'Ol, what do you want *me* for? I'm fat!' He doesn't care. Black men like big women. I mean, he wants to *marry* me, Nik. He said he's never met a woman like me in his life. Oliver's a millionaire, you know."

The salient feature of Oliver—a man I never met but spent a lot of time praying would come into our lives—was not that he was rich but that he was sober. My mother was a natural-born junkie. She lived with a consistent, daily appetite for heroin and prescription painkillers and, on special occasions—Christmas, birthdays, the 1980s—crack and cocaine. Oliver hadn't touched drugs or alcohol in more than fifteen years and had no intention of doing so again, except as a salesman.

One afternoon, as Oliver and Kathi were driving around Cape Ann, he hit the dashboard of his Lincoln and thanked my mother for buying it for him.

"Ol says to me, 'Kathi, this new house I'm buying, it's already half yours. You paid for it. If you won't marry me, won't you at least live there with me?' "

"Marry him, Mum. Do this for yourself. Please."

But my mother was already married when she met Oliver. While she was out burning money for her amusement, her husband was sitting faithfully in front of one of the two televisions that were always blaring at our house, cigarette in hand, a can of beer close by. He didn't worry about his wife driving around with another man, and he didn't need to; Kathi's marriage vows were a promise that she actually kept.

ONE SPRING MORNING IN 1986, a few days after I'd gone to the hospital to have a ring on my finger removed, I discovered the man who had driven us to the hospital sleeping next to my mother in her water bed. The skin on his back was pitted with acne scars and the breath wafting from his open mouth stank of beer. It was a weekday morning, time for me to go to school, and I knew from experience that I had a better chance of waking up this stranger than of rousing my mother. Kathi slept like the dead. I could shake and shake her but she wouldn't budge until I'd pressed ice cubes or a cold jug of milk against her leg. Even if I succeeded in waking her, there was no guarantee that she would then get up and drive me to school. And every time a "tardy" showed up on my report card another tiny ulcer seared the lining of my stomach.

"Hey." I shook the sleeping man's shoulder. His snores stopped and he looked at me with bloodshot eyes. "Hey. Can you give me a ride?"

He got up, pulled on his pants, and lit a cigarette. The car he drove was a blue Chevy Nova with one brown door. On the ride to school, Michael leaned his body toward the open window as though he might curl up and take a nap there. He drove with one hand on the wheel, the other drumming out the beat of a tune from the radio on his knee. When we got to St. Mary's, I hopped out of the car. Michael leaned out the window and called out, "Smell ya later!"

My mother dated this cabbie for about two weeks before he packed all his clothes into the back of his car and moved in with us. Four years later—on my tenth birthday—they got married.

MY MOTHER HAD CATASTROPHIC taste in men. She tried to blame this on me. "You were such a guy magnet, Nikki. They always fell in love with you first."

One of her suitors was a drug dealer named Richie. His claim to fame was that he knew a guy who knew a guy who knew George Jung, the man whose life story would one day become a movie called *Blow*, starring Johnny Depp. Richie had grand plans for my mother to smuggle cocaine for him in my diapers.

"He told me to meet him in Florida," Mum recalled years later. "He even bought you and me round-trip tickets. But I was too afraid." She made a fist with her hand and bit it anxiously. "Oh, sometimes when I think of the money we could have made, I just want to cry!"

I was too young to remember Richie. All the other boyfriends have fused into an amalgam named Raúl, a congenital scumbag who bought my mother a lot of gold necklaces, then ripped them off her neck one afternoon when they were fighting and tried to flush them down the toilet. I don't remember how old I was then, only that I openly despised Raúl and he and my mother tolerated this just fine. The morning after one of their all-night coke binges, I found a can of soda on the bathroom counter and took a swig. Flat, syrupy cigarette ashes went down my throat and quickly came back up. It was a point of pride for me as a kid that I could vomit all by myself, no assistance necessary. (My mother cried like a baby and made me rub her back whenever she puked.) I cleaned myself and the bathroom, then gleefully told my mother what had happened. I was fishing for a sympathetic yelp, maybe even a conciliatory Happy Meal.

"Fuckin' Raúl," Kathi said. But anyone could have left the can in there. It could easily have been her.

MIKE THE GREEK WAS how Kathi introduced the cabdriver to our family. He grew up in Danvers, in an apartment just across the river from my mother. His father owned a taxi company whose office and garage were next door to his home. Michael started sweeping the garage when he was eleven years old and learned auto mechanics in high school. His father treated him worse than any of the other employees, scheduling him around the clock and paying him less. It was in this garage and in the dark, wood-paneled dispatcher's office upstairs, papered with decades of crinkled porn and ripped-out comics, that Michael smoked his first cigarette and drank his first beer, probably alone.

"He grew up in a dungeon," my mother said. She felt sorrier for Michael than for anyone else in the world, including herself.

FROM THE GET-GO MIKE the Greek seemed different from my mother's other boyfriends. He was clownish and mellow when he was sober, quiet but quick to laugh when he was drunk. He loved Led Zeppelin loud and Neil Young electric. He loved the crude, stuttering freaks on *The Howard Stern Show*. He always had a working car, and he sang along to the radio with passion. By the time he took up a permanent post in my mother's water bed, I had already decided to like him.

Michael and Kathi would get high and smoke cigarettes all night in our living room. They were so happy and in love that my mother would let me stay up as late as I wanted with them. She made me my favorite mocktail—Coca-Cola on the rocks with a dash of milk. I made up funny stories to entertain them while they took turns cutting and blowing lines off our coffee table, an old wooden lobster trap with a plate of glass on top. We rented Brian De Palma's *Scarface* so many weekends in a row that the video-store owner let us keep it. Michael did an amazing impression of Pacino's Tony Montana. For a spell, he had an almost autistic tendency to talk with a Cuban accent, so much so that my mother and I started calling him Mang. When I had to leave a note for him, I would address it like this:

> *Mang,*
> *I need a ride to dance class tomorrow at 3:15!*
> *Ju got a proling with that?*
> *Love, Nikki*

My mother drove a taxi for Michael's father for almost six weeks before she quit. "I swear to Christ, I'll never work for another Greek as long as I live," she said. By then her goal had been achieved—a live-in boyfriend who helped her pay bills and didn't mind chauffeuring her daughter around town. She used the opportunity to go back to school and get her manicurist license.

As Michael's father grew older and increasingly alcoholic (the elder Greek died painfully of liver cancer in his early sixties), my stepdad became the reluctant boss of the C&A Taxi Company. It was the inheritance of a migraine. The company consisted of a small fleet of broken-down cabs serving a suburban community where nearly everyone with a driver's license owned a car. The mainstay of the taxi business was a few elderly women who could no longer make it to the supermarket and back on their own and who tipped ten cents on a five-dollar fare.

It was clear that Michael was going to run his father's business into the ground, so Kathi started hanging around the office to see if she could help. Only two of the nine cabs were running, and the accountant, a wizened old man who was himself dying of lung cancer, recommended Chapter 11. With no education, business, or even managerial experience whatsoever, my mother transformed C&A Taxi into Kathi, Inc., a coach and livery company specializing in the transport of special-needs children. She secured five- and six-figure contracts with every school district on the North Shore. She was on a first-name basis with several superintendents and town selectmen. At Christmas, our run-down little house would be filled with gourmet fruit baskets from various school committees and PTAs. Within a few short years, my mother's new company was grossing a million dollars a year.

"Nikki," she said, "your mother is literally a millionaire."

Millionaire became Kathi's favorite word. She dropped it into every conversation, telling anyone who would listen how much money she made and spent in a given day. Coming from her demographic, it was hard for Kathi to understand money as the abstraction that it is. Saving, investing—these things were not within her ken. Profligate spending, however, was a talent she'd perfected long before she had the capital to fund it. While Michael sat on the living-room couch watching NASCAR races and drinking Budweiser, my mother and I went shopping. She bought me a calfskin trench coat the color of crème brûlée that cost what I now, as an adult who lives alone, pay for one month's rent. Since the day she bought it for me more than ten years ago, I've worn it only twice. Both times, I couldn't look at myself in the mirror without imagining a bullet ripping through the buttery leather and staining the beautiful coat with my blood. She bought my college boyfriend, now a filmmaker, his first professional-quality video camera. I had my own American Express card attached to her account, which she encouraged me to use whenever I liked. The lie I told myself was that Mum's credit card was for emergencies only. Every time I got into a fight with her, I declared an emotional state of emergency and took my boyfriend out to dinner.

For my college graduation present she flew us to Paris. I don't remember much about this trip besides blowing my mother's Oxy-

Contins and puking in front of the Eiffel Tower. For our last full day in France, I sobered up and demanded that we go to the Louvre. Kathi got good and high before we left, and for the first twenty minutes she walked around the museum with a truly inspiring sense of wonder. I remember watching her approach an early Christian painting of the Madonna and Child. She got so close that I was afraid she would reach out and touch the canvas. I held my breath and scanned the perimeter for both exits and security guards.

Kathi stepped back and laughed. "Look at his little dinky!" she cried.

I ushered her to another room filled with Greco-Roman statues. My mother shrugged. "Either there's a head without a body or a body without a head." She was coming down from her high, growing much harder to impress. When she sat on a bench to rest, I was relieved. For the moment, Kathi was at a safe distance from any work of art. I looked at some of the statues, forcing myself to think sophisticated thoughts about them, always glancing back at my mother to check on her. Right there on a bench in the middle of a grand hall in the Louvre, Kathi pulled a little straw out of her shirt pocket and an OxyContin that she had crushed up and saved in a folded scrap of paper. I watched her blow it up her nose while sitting in the eminent shadow of the *Winged Victory of Samothrace.*

"What?" she cried when she caught me gaping at her. "We're in France, for Christ's sake. Why are you always so concerned with what other people think?"

We never made it to Versailles, but my mother had obviously been inspired by her trip abroad, because when we got home from Paris she decided to build an addition on our house. This process necessitated home inspections from town bureaucrats, who not only said that we couldn't build an addition but, after seeing the holes in the floor and the rats nesting between the walls, had our house condemned by the Department of Health. Mum said *fine,* then *fuck it* and had the whole house torn down so that she could build a new one in its place. During the next few months, a structure three times the size of the old house was built. Part of me never believed it would be finished, or that my mother would live long enough to move in. Kathi's Xanadu, I called it.

It was painful for Michael, a tall goofy guy always lurking at the edge of the room, to see the business he despised and was determined to destroy flourish in the hands of his bold, ambitious wife. The more she and the business succeeded, the more he drank. He started drinking in the mornings, and stealing my mother's painkillers. She knew that he was stealing from her and was hurt only by the fact that he didn't just ask her for them. Of course she would have said yes. My mother had to hire another mechanic to follow Michael around the garage and fix his shoddy work. Mang still dispatched sometimes, sitting in the dark, wood-paneled office surrounded by those same old comic strips, the same old pinup girls splayed across the hood of a hot rod, the paper now curled into crispy yellow flakes from thousands of cigarettes smoked by my parents and their employees. Sometimes he drove a van full of special-needs kids to and from school, though he should never have been allowed behind the wheel of a car. At night he sat alone in the living room watching TV, putting together model cars and huffing the glue.

Kathi once told me that she and Michael had no sex life. "Like none whatsoever," she said. How does any daughter respond to that? Die a small death, then search for a silver lining—I hoped that the ritual of shooting heroin together was at least tender for them.

I CAME HOME FROM boarding school, and later from college, to find brown scars of cigarette burns on our living-room couch spreading like a pox. One summer I lifted a towel off the armrest and discovered that a large chunk of the sofa was charred. My mother told me about the night that she smelled smoke from her bedroom, and went to the living room to find that Michael had nodded off and the arm of the couch engulfed in flames.

"He was still sleeping after I threw a pan of water on him," she said. "I was so fucking mad I almost beat him to death with the pan. That was a brand-new couch!"

As long as I had known Michael, he had been trying to kill himself just cowardly enough that he would live another day. I realized this one night in our old house when I was eleven or twelve. I had been woken up again by my stepfather's snores. It was a loud inhuman sound, as if rocks and tar were tumbling in his chest. I heard him cough himself awake, then blunder down the hall to the bathroom, where he never bothered to shut the door. I pressed my eyes shut and listened to the clunk of the toilet lid being lifted and then all those tar-covered rocks being summoned in an efflux of vomit. Heaving. Liquids splashing. The flush of the toilet followed by Michael's footsteps down the hall and around the corner to the kitchen. The seal of the refrigerator door opened and the hum of its motor groaned as though irritated at being woken up. The crack of a Budweiser, the hiss of carbonation, the sound of swallowing punctuated by gasps and grunts. The fridge door shut, feet shuffled back to bed, and the snore returned.

I loved my stepfather, and so I had to dehumanize him a little in order to witness his slow-motion suicide. I began ignoring him whenever I visited, deleting him from the scene, so that now when I try to recall certain events of my past I wonder whether Michael was even there. The sight of him, his pitted gray skin, his shaky hand holding a Budweiser, his big stomach lopped over a pair of sweatpants cut into shorts, his naked chest broken out in large red welts—it was one trouble too many.

I mean *he*. He was.

During my twenties, I tried to limit my time at my mother's house to three-hour sessions. I would spend that time binge-eating, and if I didn't get too high on my mother's pills I would clean her house with a martyr's zeal. I breezed past Michael as I collected empty cigarette packs and moldy plates of food, either saying nothing to my stepfather or passive-aggressively muttering my disappointments under my breath, as though he were an inert lump of flesh and I had all the answers.

"He's the kindest man you'll ever meet if you can catch him before noon" was my mother's wifely refrain.

It was true. Without Michael, I would not have gotten to school most mornings. Some of the best memories of my childhood are of my stepdad driving me to St. Mary's. For those ten minutes, he was sober and alive in a way few people got to see him. But even when he was drunk I couldn't help loving him. There were many lonely nights when my mother was still at work or passed out in her bedroom that I turned to Michael to get me through that knotted shred of darkness, the hours after the sun disappeared but before my eyes got tired. I could rely on my stepfather to be sitting on the same spot of the couch watching something I would like on TV. We must have watched *The Godfather* together at least a hundred times, so that now, in my reimagined childhood, that movie is playing in the background on a perpetual loop.

Michael Corleone stands over the baptismal font as the priest christens his baby nephew, while his enemies are exterminated in a violent waltz across the screen. Mang and Nikki clap and cheer at each new murder in a living room hazy with smoke. Michael Corleone goes to Sicily, marries a young girl who is blown up in a car before his eyes. Nikki grows up, starts smoking Mang's cigarettes, starts drinking his beers. "I didn't want this for you," he says to her. "Congressman Ruta. Senator Ruta . . ."

YEARS AND YEARS LATER, after everything was lost, after she was gone for good, and I had fucked up my own life in more ways than I could count, I would follow a friend's sweet tooth into our local Dunkin' Donuts. I stood by with mild impatience as my friend ordered a bag of chocolate Munchkins from the man behind the counter. The man in the brown uniform with the pink-and-orange nametag kept staring at me, hardly blinking. I was on the verge of snapping "What do you want?" when I heard the clerk call me by name. That voice, gentle and hoarse.

"Michael?"

My friend told me later, "Your face just crumpled like a piece of paper." It had been more than five years since I'd seen my stepfather. What was I supposed to do? What was I supposed to say?

"Can I have a hug, Mang?"

"You betcha!"

Michael came out from behind the counter and lifted me up in his arms. My feet were dangling off the ground and I had to wipe my eyes and nose on my sleeve.

"Come see my new bike," he said.

I followed him outside. The twentysomething woman acting as his manager sniffed indignantly. Michael waved his hand without turning to look at her and said, "I'm taking five."

On the sidewalk, he showed me his two proudest possessions—a bright-blue Schwinn chained to a tree and a full set of dentures in his mouth. "The teeth are brand-new, but the bike is used." He rapped on his teeth with his knuckles. They were perfectly square and white. "Pretty cool, huh?"

"Michael, I'm so sorry. You have no idea how sorry I am. . . ."

"*Shhhhh!*" he said, and hugged me again. "I always hoped I'd run into you one day."

BUT BEFORE ALL THAT, in my freshman year of high school, the last year I lived at home, Michael and I went to see *Tommy* at the Shubert Theatre in Boston. The show was on a school night and both of us got dressed up—jeans and a tie for him, jeans and a blouse for me. Michael, who had been drinking since noon, as usual, and was already pretty loaded, downed a six-pack of Budweiser on the drive in. We picked up our tickets at a bar called the Penalty Box, where we stayed for another beer. When we left the bar, Michael tried to hold my hand as we crossed the street. The feeling of his sweaty palm against mine nauseated me. I pulled my hand away dramatically, a gesture that left an instant and visible wound on him. I watched him dash to the nearest convenience store and buy a sixteen-ounce beer, which he drank from a paper bag as we hurried to the theater. I felt awful. I knew that I should reach for his hand again, that I should find a way to apologize.

"Come on, we're late," I said instead, and we broke into a silent run.

At fourteen, I considered myself a pretty discerning judge of what passed for good theater, and that night's production of *Tommy* was amazing. Roger Daltrey was sitting in the audience not far from us. Or so Michael said. His blood-alcohol content was in the whole numbers by the time we took our seats. The lights went up and the opening chords of the overture filled the auditorium. Out of the corner of my eye, I saw my stepdad reach for his cigarettes then put them back, remembering with bemusement where he was. But he couldn't stop himself from dancing in his seat, from pumping his fist, playing air guitar, and drumming on his knees. Everyone around us was quiet and still, but Michael was rocking out.

At one point he turned to me and said much too loudly, "I don't get it. Why is everybody just sitting here?"

"Michael, it's a play, not a concert," I whispered.

"But it's the fuckin' Who."

He was right. He was totally right. I wish more than anything that I had told him so.

The Curse

MY MOTHER WAS ALWAYS HOUNDING ME TO GET PREGNANT WHILE I was still in high school. It was an easy favor to refuse. Sex looked like an awful lot of work to me, whereas chastity was a virtue I could fulfill while lounging in front of the TV. Although I wasn't quite a virgin, I did enjoy the romantic fantasies of all young girls who have yet to fall in love. Lying in bed, I dreamed up draft after draft of a fantasy boyfriend, a swarthy hybrid of this tall, lanky guy in my English class spliced with Johnny Depp and Huck Finn, an erotic imaginary friend who, like me, loved Shakespeare and Toni Morrison and, like Huck Finn, knew how to build a fire and gut a fish. This dream boy and I would go for long, romantic walks in a mythical wilderness, and when we found the perfect spot we'd stop and make out for hours.

In real life, when a guy at school got up the courage to ask me out on a date, I immediately assumed the worst—it's a joke, it's a plot, he's a lunatic who's going to kill me, kill me and *then* rape me, or manipulate me into writing his English paper for him.

I didn't have a real boyfriend until my junior year in high school. The smart, WASPy Andover boys were intimidating, with their squash racquets and their acoustic guitars, so I settled for a suburban pothead named Steve. I'd met him through my friend Julie over Thanksgiving break that year. Together we went on long walks in the woods of Hamilton and when we found the perfect spot we'd stop and smoke a joint.

Steve and I dry-humped for about six months straight, until we wore holes in our jeans. Then there was the rainy unromantic Easter weekend that my mother and Michael went away to Martha's Vineyard and left Steve and me alone to watch the house. Between us we had no car, no driver's license, no job, and no money. How else were we supposed to entertain ourselves?

When my mother returned, she knew right away that I had had sex. She walked into my bedroom and hoped out loud that I was pregnant. Shortly afterward, I had my annual physical. When the nurse called me in, my mother got up and followed me into the examining room. It was rare that she even accompanied me to the doctor's. Usually a cab dropped me off at my appointments, and when they were over I called another cab to pick me up. My mother sat in a leather chair, and I turned my back to her as I got into a paper gown. When the doctor came in, Kathi hopped up and said, "Nikki wants to go on the pill," then scooted out of the examining room and down the hall. It would take me twenty minutes after my physical to realize that she had left me there, and it was another two hours before a cab came to take me home.

Kathi contradicted this moment of maternal intuition just a few days later. "You know, Honey, if you just skipped a pill every once in a while Mummy wouldn't be mad at you at all," she said in a cloying, babyish voice, as though trying to appeal to a much younger, more easily manipulated version of me.

I rolled my eyes. "I'm applying to colleges."

"Oh, that's okay, Sweetie. You can still go to school. Mummy will take care of the baby. You wouldn't have to do a thing."

She was thirty-seven years old and could never again have children because of the hysterectomy she had had in the prime of her reproductive years. She knew that I was moving further away from her, and her body longed for something small and witless to cuddle. I should have been more sympathetic, but the pleasure I took in saying no to her felt even more liberating than my new sex life.

"Not gonna happen, Mum."

"Oh!" She stomped her foot. "Why can't you be just a little less responsible?"

———

WHEN I WAS A young girl, my mother tried to drill into me a pragmatic, almost mercenary concept of love. She had an ongoing lecture series for me, her audience of one, which always delivered the same message: smart women never marry for love; they marry for money. "I wish I was smart like you," she'd say. Her eyes would roll up toward the sky and she'd fold her hands above my head and pray out loud, "Dear God, please don't let my daughter fall for a man with limited education or seasonal employment."

Sometime during her sober, back-to-school endeavors, Kathi took me to see Gloria Steinem, who was giving a reading at the local state college. Steinem talked about the revolution that can happen when people share their deepest secrets with one another. It was one of those moments, instantaneous as a chemical reaction: I could feel myself changing. After the applause, Mum pushed me to the front of the auditorium. "Go introduce yourself to her."

"No. Why?"

"So she can know who Nikki Ruta is."

It was a school night, so I said something about having homework to finish and we left. On the drive home my mother talked about the books she was reading at Harvard, and this somehow turned into another lecture about love and marriage.

"If I could do it all over I'd marry a much older man," she said. "Someone rich. Someone who would die early in the marriage." She pulled a cigarette out of her pack, a long, minty Newport 100, and lit it with the end of the cigarette that was still in her mouth. She tossed the old butt out the window, and I turned to watch it. A tiny orange gem fell backward, smashed into the blacktop, and broke into even tinier sparks that quickly disappeared in the road behind us.

"You'll be different." Mum looked at me for a second and smiled. "You're smart, so you'll make your own money."

"I intend to."

"But that has its problems, too."

"What do you mean?"

"Men don't like a woman who's *too* independent. Or too smart."

"Uh-oh."

"Don't worry, Hon. You won't have any trouble attracting men. You have that smell, and that look in your eyes. The women in our family are very fertile. Men can smell that. They like it, too, even if they don't think they do."

I knew she was right, but I didn't want to admit it. Even though I wasn't conventionally pretty, at St. Mary's I'd always been the girl that the boys wanted to stand next to in line. Somehow they knew they could lift up my skirt, sneak a sweaty palm down my panties, and squeeze, and though I would gasp and my eyes would burn with hot, stifled tears, I wouldn't let myself cry, and I would *never* tell on them. If there was an indecent exposure at the food court in the mall, you'd better believe the lecher in the sweatpants chose the table next to mine to whip out his greasy hamster of a dick. It was as if my body hummed at a pitch that only the most desperate men could hear. I wheezed a secret dog whistle to the soulless and the depraved. But this phenomenon wasn't a secret if even my mother knew about it, and here she was describing it as a smell, not a sound. It called to mind the wet nose of a Doberman pressed into my crotch.

"Mum, that's so gross."

"What? I'm telling you the truth."

FOUR YEARS LATER, MY mother's story had completely changed. As Kathi approached forty, her ambitions and ideals for both of us were fast corroding. "You can't choose who you fall in love with," she now told me. "Love is a curse. An awful, miserable curse. And once you're in it you can never get yourself out."

MY FIRST BOYFRIEND, STEVE, had strawberry-blond hair and full, pink lips, and wore large, billowing jeans that sagged below his waist.

He went to Hamilton High, where he bragged about sometimes dropping acid in homeroom.

"How is that even fun?" I asked him. I couldn't imagine anything worse than an acid trip under fluorescent lighting and the suspicious glares of my teachers.

It must have offended him, because he quickly changed the subject. "You have the biggest calves I've ever seen on a girl. Seriously, they're huge."

Steve rivaled my mother in his ability to build me up and tear me to shreds in a single breath. "I love you," he told me, "because you're homely and smart. I've dated beautiful girls. But you're so much more fun."

I flew to him like a bird caught in a blizzard, not knowing which way is up, and I soared headlong into the ground. For a year and a half, I loved this boy with my every cell and no sense at all. He insulted me in public and pushed me around, and eventually dumped me for a girl in the eighth grade, whom he took to his senior prom. I know this because my mother lent him a car for the big night, as well as the money for a tux and his date's corsage. I found pictures that Kathi had taken of Steve and his child date on her dresser one day while I was scavenging for pills. The pictures were clearly taken on our porch, with a view of the river behind the happy couple. I tore the photos up and threw them conspicuously in the trash can next to Mum's bed.

Kathi was furious. "That wasn't very nice of you, Nikki," she said. "Steve wanted me to have those pictures. Steve's my friend! Just because you're done with him doesn't mean I am."

She must have forgotten that Steve was the one who'd broken up with me. I was so deranged by love that I would have stayed with this boy for the rest of my life. It was New Year's Day 1997. I leaned in to kiss him, and he turned to me and said, "I've changed my mind. I don't love you anymore." I begged him to take me back, and when he said no, I puked uncontrollably until my mother gave me a Xanax. I sobbed for the remainder of winter vacation and into the start of the new semester. I couldn't eat, having no appetite for anything but vodka, which I drank straight out of a plastic bottle that I stored in my dresser, sometimes first thing in the morning.

All this must have slipped my mother's mind.

Because that following spring, Kathi hired Steve to be her assistant at the taxi company that she had just begun to take over. She spent every day with him. He was her right-hand man. Mum claimed that Steve was "wicked smart, a genius at the computer." In my mother's eyes, an ability to open and close a spreadsheet qualified as technical wizardry; the only thing I ever saw Steve do on a computer was simulate combat in some gory video game. He was barely passing his remedial classes at school. This wasn't because he had dyslexia or ADD or a disadvantaged background, all of which are legitimate roadblocks to academic success. He was just really stupid. I remember the crushing moment when I was forced to admit this to myself. We had just finished having sex for the third time (I was still counting) when a song came on the radio, "Paint It Black," by the Rolling Stones.

"Do you know what it's about?" Steve asked me.

We'd turned the music up loud to cover the sound of my squeaky mattress and I didn't hear him. "What?" I asked.

"This song. It's about depression," he said instructively. Steve had had some dark and beautiful thoughts in his life, but this one was the biggest. "It's, like, sometimes, the lyrics to a song are saying one thing, but they actually mean something else."

I found my underwear balled up at the foot of the bed and pulled them back on, then lay down with my head on Steve's chest. He patted my face, and I felt my heart sinking. Here was obviously the only boy who would ever love me in my entire life, and this was his intellectual big bang.

Steve was the kind of person who would wait until his friends passed out drunk, then rifle the cash from their wallets. If he stole from his own friends, you can imagine his ethics regarding an employer. In the end, he funneled tens of thousands of dollars from my mother's cab company. But in the beginning he was just a petty scam artist who used to fill up his friends' gas tanks on my mother's company account, then pocket their cash. Clever as this scam was, he wasn't smart enough to keep his mouth shut. I heard through mutual friends what was going on, and mirthfully reported it to my mother.

"I'm disgusted with you, Nikki," Kathi said. "I didn't think *my daughter* would ever turn into a rat." She shot me a look so hateful that I trembled. "And at least Steve helps me! It's not like I can count on you to come home and help me with the family business."

She was right. Despite her pleas and outright demands, I didn't drop out of boarding school or college to come home, have illegitimate babies, and run the taxi business for her. To punish me, she gave Steve a car, and after he wrecked it she bought him another one. She took him and his various girlfriends on vacation with her and Michael to Florida. Sometimes she let him live in my bedroom while I was away at college.

"Whose bra is this?" I'd ask my mother as I sorted through a heap of laundry piled up on the bathroom floor. The bra in question was definitely not mine, and it was much too small to be my mother's.

"Oh, that must be Allison's," Mum said. "Steve's girlfriend. She's a tiny little thing."

I always knew who had been sleeping in my bedroom by what had been left behind. Condoms and drugstore cologne meant Steve; crack pipes and porn on VHS meant my stepfather. There were several occasions on which my mother let Uncle Vic sleep in my bed when Auntie Lucy threw him out.

"You know that Uncle Vic is a child molester," I said to my mother. I was home on vacation and putting the pillows and sheets his body had touched through their third round in the washing machine.

"You know that he—"

"Oh, Honey, no," my mother interrupted. "Please! I don't want to believe that. I love Uncle Vic. He's such a good guy." Her knees buckled. She looked like a little kid who needed to pee but was waiting for permission to go. "And Mummy owes him a lot of money right now, so I'm not exactly in a position to argue. Okay?"

Heat waves rippled my mother's face, her body, the knotted wood paneling of the hallway where she stood. I saw these things quiver as though through a bonfire, and in an instant the entire house went up in silent black flames. Disappeared, sucked backward at the speed of sound and dropped for one heartbeat in the past. Those last few words were familiar. Mum's exact tone of voice, pleading, desperate, almost resentful that I would even suggest . . . When had I heard those lines before? Maybe as a kid? I couldn't remember in any logical or narrative sense, but I could hear a warped feedback echoing inside my chest.

Don't ask me to protect you right now, because I can't afford to. Okay?

No, that didn't happen.

I came back. I was in my bedroom again. The emerald-green walls, the taxi-yellow door, my short, lumpy mother posed inside the doorframe like a distorted work of art.

IT DIDN'T MATTER, I decided after a couple of beers. I had turned eighteen and gotten another scholarship to a small college in Ohio called Oberlin. I would have dropped out the first week if it weren't for the massive quantity of drugs available on campus. What I remember most about college is eating mescaline and mushrooms with trust-fund kids, and smoking opium on a bunk bed in a dorm. I recently combed my journal from those years hoping to find something worth writing about. I found nothing but the illegible notes from one of my acid trips.

My mother would mail me one or two of her OxyContins every month. "Just in case you get bad cramps," she'd say. In all my years as a menstruating woman I have never once had cramps, and my mother knew this. I would open my care packages in the student mailroom and run to the bathroom to snort an Oscar off the back of a toilet tank. The sleaziness of it was half the fun. It was another role I was trying to play, and playing badly—the cool, mysterious addict. Nobody was fooled. Even with the crumbs of opiates packed into my nostrils, I was way too high-strung to be considered cool by any-one.

Oberlin was like an extended summer camp for aspiring drug ad-dicts. Everyone had ADD, and, even if they didn't, a quick doctor's visit between classes could get you a diagnosis and a prescription for Ritalin or Adderall. The college had an extremely lax policy regard-ing marijuana. Kids in my dorm who got caught with four-foot pot plants growing in their closet were punished with two weeks of com-munity service—mowing the lawns, spreading mulch around trees, stuff like that. In the end, they would actually learn how to grow a hardier plant.

Since I was no longer afraid of getting kicked out, as I had been at Andover, there was nothing to stop me from getting drunk or high whenever I liked. Smoking pot forced me to exhale, which led to the mistaken conclusion that I was relaxed. By the end of my first semes-ter at college, this drug-induced tranquility had quickly cascaded to resignation. All ambitions drained away. I didn't want to be a doctor or to liberate political prisoners. I didn't even care if I got a C in his-tory. For the first time in my life, I didn't care about anything, and it felt wonderful. Once or twice a week, I would grace my professors with my presence. Most of the time I wandered the woods in a hal-lucinogenic stupor. When midterms or finals came, I would trade an OxyContin for someone else's Ritalin or Adderall and make up months of work in one blinkless night.

What did I learn in college? How to write a bullshit twelve-page Marxist critique of a book I never opened. How to grind my teeth quietly when a coke binge with so-called friends got too tense. How to persuade a doctor to write me a year's prescription for Xanax. How to alienate myself from nice people and assholes alike. How to get through the day without ever touching the ground or soaring above it, either. How to get by.

My only achievement at Oberlin was entrapping a really hand-some boyfriend. Dave was a smart, sensitive Jewish boy from Missis-sippi. He could juggle three apples and take a bite out of one while it was still in the air. He was a chess master, a talented artist, and a pretty good basketball player. To make me smile, he would moonwalk across the floor of the library like Michael Jackson. When he laughed, his cheeks dimpled. He was the most beautiful boy I had ever seen. One night I tossed a forty-ounce bottle of Olde English off the roof of our dorm, grabbed him by the collar, and made him kiss me. The moon was so full that it looked too big to hang there in the sky without falling. Two weeks later, Dave and I moved in together. We spent the following semester in a tiny twin bed where we hardly ever slept. People in our dorm would bang on the walls and shout at us to be quiet. Dave turned up the music on his stereo and we'd keep going. I wish everyone could know a first love like this.

After four years, it was time to graduate. This was a big deal in my family, as no one had ever done that before. Everyone flew out to witness the momentous occasion—my dad and his family, my mother and Michael. On the morning of my graduation, I was hungover as usual. Dave had recently confessed to cheating on me. His infidelity was at least half my fault, if not more. One night a couple of months earlier, he drank a few beers at a poker game, which was rare for him, as he hardly ever drank. When he came home we started to kiss and something inside me snapped. The scent of beer on his breath and the prickle of hair on his face sent a shudder that ripped through my head straight down to the sore spot between my legs.

I had been cursed. A fairy-tale explanation, it was the only thing that made sense to me. I was being punished because I was too happy, too much in love.

"What's happening to me?" I asked Dave. I had woken up from a sound sleep screaming in his bed. Again. We went for a walk to the playground near his house and I confessed, "I can't tell whether it's real or just a bad dream I keep having." He knew exactly what was happening. He'd met my family, he'd been to my house. He wasn't surprised at all, only heartbroken—for me and for us.

From that moment on, sex had as much appeal to me as sticking a rusty needle in a gangrenous wound. I did anything to avoid it.

Nagged, bitched, fought, complained, got black-out drunk, and puked, finally pushing this sweet, handsome boyfriend as far away as I could.

On the morning of graduation day I still hadn't decided if I was going to kill Dave, forgive him, or run away to Moscow. I didn't even know where I was going after graduation. We had a lease together for an off-campus house that was running out in a couple of days. My mother's house was a hoarder's prison, and I was sick of trying to clean it. My father had a kid in every bedroom and his elderly mother squeezed into the corner of the living room behind a bookcase, so there was no room for me there. I didn't have a job. Gainful employment was one of many items on a long list of "Things I'd Rather Not Think About." Between drinking, fighting, nursing hangovers, and making up, who had time to write a résumé?

I stood in front of my bathroom mirror that morning and swiped some mascara on my eyelashes. *What the fuck am I going to do?* I asked myself. As if on cue, my mother arrived at my house armed with a hairbrush and a curling iron. We'd decided the night before that she would do my hair and, surprisingly, she had remembered. The woman had brilliant timing, I could never deny her that. She stood in the bathroom doorway while I smudged concealer under my eyes. I braced myself for some criticism, but she didn't say anything for a long time. She just watched me.

"Honey," she said softly. "Here—"

I looked at her and she offered me a plate with a little straw and a crushed-up OxyContin raked into a line.

Was this a bad idea? I wondered. Could she tell that I was scared? Was this the paradox of a junkie's love, the only way she knew to help? Or was this an initiation rite? Was my mother now taking over the next phase of my education, molding me into the kind of woman she had become, a sporadically functioning addict? Was she really that sick? Was I? What was going to happen to us now?

It was too much to think about. I took the plate from her and snorted my line.

"You know, you can snort it into your mouth, too," she said.

"What?"

"Mummy does it like this," she told me. I watched her put the little straw between her lips and suck up what was left.

"Why?"

"I have to do it that way now. But I think it's better. The thing in between my nostrils—the?"

"Septum?"

"The septum. It's not there anymore."

"Oh."

We forgot about my hair and walked toward campus together. I don't remember what we talked about. My head was no longer a solid thing but a delicate cloud of gas. I walked slowly, careful of every step. I imagined kicking a rock, the imperceptible spark as the rock skidded across the pavement, and *kaboom*! The wrong word, the faintest breath, could blow up the sky.

I floated away from my mother to my alphabetically assigned seat where immediately I nodded off. An hour or so later, a stranger shook my shoulder. He told me to get up. My name had been called and I had missed it.

HAVING NO BETTER PLACE to go, I moved to Boston after graduation and took my college boyfriend hostage. I found a temporary job as a clerk in a bookstore, and Dave worked the night shift at an artisanal bakery. He would come home at three in the morning with warm bags of bread—sourdoughs and olive rolls and baguettes. It was all we ate. Our work schedules were misaligned, so that I had to do all the grocery shopping alone, and after the second or third winter blizzard I gave up. There was bread to eat, olive oil and salt to season it, and a liquor store that sold pistachios for protein. I'd line my sneakers with plastic shopping bags and trudge to the liquor store on the corner, where I bought either a bottle of scotch or a six-pack of beer every other day. Many days were so cold that I couldn't leave the apartment unless I was already drunk.

Dave's parents, both lawyers, were disconcerted by the downward economic trajectory their son's post-college life was taking. My parents wondered out loud what had been the point of a college education. "Kids in high school can ring up sales at a cash register," Kathi crowed, then wrote me a check for the first and last month's rent and the security deposit for our apartment. When the rental company rejected her credit report, Dave's parents co-signed our lease.

"Honey, listen to Mummy," Kathi told me. "Have Dave's baby *now*. Before he finds someone better than you."

While I didn't get pregnant, an unnatural domestication took place. Kids my age were going to rock shows, getting ironic tattoos, and hopping from one hip romance to another. I was pretending to be a married woman, doing laundry and cooking dinner. Dave balanced the checkbook, got the tires rotated, and fixed leaky faucets. Weekday mornings, as I stood at the kitchen sink rinsing out last night's beer bottles, I would be seized by the sensation of a hand on my throat. Sometimes I could shake it off with a shot of scotch, which I kept in a crystal decanter on the counter, but the feeling never fully disappeared. It hovered in my apartment, in the grocery store, in the gym, where I killed myself with sit-ups, haunting me with questions I couldn't answer.

"When is it going to happen?" I would whisper as I washed the dishes. When was *what* going to happen? I had no idea.

When I finally got a real job, I thought, Well, *that* must be it. It wasn't, but I was distracted for the moment, and earning a bit more money. I was hired as an activities coordinator in the Alzheimer and Dementia unit of a nursing home. For eight hours a day I played the hapless leader to a dozen lost souls, men and women who'd led lives of dignity and now looked to me, a twenty-something-year-old stranger, to remind them who and where they were. I kept them busy with a kindergartenish program of finger painting and sing-alongs. Every day at sundown the old folks went berserk. One woman would put on her hat and coat and sit by the locked door, clutching an empty purse tightly against her chest as she waited for her mother to pick her up.

"What did you do to her?" a man once blurted in the middle of our daily exercise class. He was holding a three-pound hand weight that he was ready to hurl at me. "What did you do to my mother?"

Others had lost their ability to speak and simply howled.

Every morning I would sit them down at the activities table with mugs of decaf. Even though I knew how all twelve of them took their coffee, I went through the ritual of asking them again. It always made them feel good to remember a simple script like "Cream, no sugar." Sometimes we played bingo. I would pluck out numbers from a rotating wire basket as the old folks peered at their cards without making a move. Because they loved bingo, and always perked up when I started a game, I had to memorize twelve different bingo cards, which I dealt to the same people each week, and play all twelve games in my head simultaneously while calling numbers.

Is it possible to have nostalgia for a time in which you never lived? I'm sure there is a word for this phenomenon in German—beautiful, absurd, and twenty letters long. I felt more at home playing bingo and listening to Artie Shaw records with a bunch of white-haired old wraiths than I ever did with my high-school or college friends. Here was the generation I belonged to: they loved to clip coupons for food they would never buy and complain about the exorbitant price of shoes. They could sit for hours listening to stories read out loud, and they'd learned the canon of American poetry by heart. Every once in a while, when we were sitting at the activities table for our tenth coffee break of the day, I would offer a single line:

"The woods are lovely, dark, and deep. . . ."

Like a pebble tossed in the still water of a koi pond, memories rippled out of them in concentric circles.

"And I have promises to keep."

"And miles to go before I sleep."

"And miles to go before I sleep."

I didn't play with poetry often, because it always made me cry, and tears are contagious in a nursing home. The residents mimicked whatever mood I was in. If I laughed, they laughed whether or not they got the joke, and if I started crying, a box of Kleenex worked its way around the table.

"Your job is so sad," Dave would say when I told him how my day went. "I don't know how you do it."

I drank, that's how. Two to three liters of scotch a week, usually alone, as Dave wasn't much of a drinker. To slow myself down I'd buy a six-pack of beer, the logic being that since I didn't really like beer this would force me to drink less. I wasn't an alcoholic. I had a job, a boyfriend, and a college diploma. It was medicinal drinking, something classy people do in *New Yorker* stories. *It's not my fault,* I would say defensively to no one but myself. Some people couldn't open their eyes before drinking a pot of coffee. I hated caffeine. I just needed one, at most two, shots of scotch to face the day. And, besides, I worked hard. Didn't I have a right to drink?

Sad as my day job was, I loved it. I felt completely at home in that place, where life was stripped down to the barest elements. Emotions in the dementia ward rose up, exploded, and cooled like the same forces of nature that formed the universe. People screamed when they were angry. They cried when they were sad. The laughter in those rooms was made of a hard, indestructible material, something mined from the deepest recesses of the human heart. We laughed a lot. Even an aphasic could tell a good joke. One woman named Leah swiped a pickle from a man's plate at lunch and regarded it curiously for a moment. She then looked at me, held the pickle at her crotch, and swung it around. Leah was seventy-two years old and had lost the ability to form a sentence, but she knew one thing instinctually:

PICKLE = PENIS = COMEDY

Leah was shorter than I was and wore unintentionally hip polyester pantsuits. I loved her to pieces. But my favorite person in the ward was a ninety-seven-year-old man named Saul. He was a hunchback with a shock of milky white hair and large blue eyes that still glimmered with understanding. Once the head of surgery at a famous

New York hospital, Saul had enjoyed decades of comfortable retirement before finding himself stranded in our unit. He spent most of his days hiding behind a *New York Times* that he would snatch from the nursing home's library. Staff and residents from the main unit were constantly asking me about this.

"Did that man steal the paper again?"

"Who, Saul?" I would say. "Impossible. He's been with me all morning."

Saul didn't have Alzheimer's, as far as I could tell. He was able to recall in startling detail a time when the Bronx was a hamlet that brushed up against wilderness, when traveling a relatively short distance was unthinkable if you didn't own a horse. He knew that there was a war going on in the Middle East, that it was suspiciously similar to another war we'd fought there not long before, and that war was a terrible thing even when it seemed just. Yet there were certain facts of his personal life that he had blocked out. His wife of sixty years had died a few years earlier; his healthy forty-year-old daughter had died very suddenly not long after his wife; his only surviving child had left him there to live the last of his days among strangers. When quizzed by specialists at the nursing home about these events, Saul would draw a blank, become very confused, and change the subject.

It made sense to me. There are some things that we have to forget about in order to get through the day.

Saul could be forgetful about other, less dramatic facts, too, but for him this seemed to be more of a lifestyle choice. He refused to remember the names of the other residents, for example, but that was because he didn't like them. They were a band of lunatics, he told me one afternoon. "I mean, they've really lost their minds!"

When certain old women in our ward got upset, they could be soothed almost instantly by being given a lifelike baby doll to hold. These dolls and all their blankets and bibs were stored in a plastic box in my office. I felt that the dolls, like Valium, should be dispensed only in an emergency. The women would swaddle the babies and hold them expertly against their breasts. Their voices would become very soft and tender as they stared into the painted, unchanging faces. Saul was horrified by these scenes.

"Are these women soft?" he asked me. "Those aren't real babies! They're dolls—am I right?"

I agreed that it was one of the creepier activities going on in our unit. I usually asked one of the nurses' aides to distribute the dolls for me, because I couldn't bring myself to pretend that the babies were real. It was too much, a line I wouldn't cross. Until a particularly bad day, when all the residents were belligerent and wailing as though possessed by a wild, bewitching moon. I treated myself to a couple of cocktails at lunch—Bloody Marys, because they counted as a serving of vegetables. When I got back to work, the residents were still raging. I surrendered and decided to open the box myself. Holding a doll in my arms, I approached a group of women who were staring blankly at their coffee mugs.

"Oh, wookit da baby!" I cried. "Ooochie cooochie coo."

The women looked at the doll and their faces lit up with sheepish glee. Just then I felt a tap on my shoulder. Saul was standing behind me. He lifted a gnarled and shaky finger up to my face. His skin was very pale and flooded with thick veins.

"Et tu, Brute?" he said.

I could not have loved anyone more.

I'd been working at the nursing home for more than a year when Saul went into the hospital with pneumonia. A few days after Christmas, I was reviewing the logbook at the beginning of my shift and read, "On December —, the ——— family reported that Saul has expired." *Expired?* Beneath this were the usual reports of what the other residents had eaten and what their bowel movements had been like. I was furious. His family hadn't felt it necessary to tell us, the nursing-home staff who'd spent all day and night with him, until after his body had been taken to New York for burial. If there was any kind of memorial service, we weren't invited.

I stormed down the hall to Saul's bedroom. The door was unlocked, and I went inside. The blinds were shut but sunlight poured in at the edges and crawled around the windowsill in stubborn, shattered rays. Everything was neat and orderly, just as Saul kept it. There were his spare set of glasses on the dresser, his pile of annotated newspapers and magazines, a little mangled by his shaky hands but neatly stacked on a chair by his bed. Beneath them lay an atlas he had borrowed, permanently, from the library, bookmarked with little scraps of paper to the pages he'd been studying, mostly of Asia and the Middle East.

I wanted something of his to keep. I felt that I deserved it. If Saul had known that he was leaving, he would have given me a token himself. (My God, I realized, we never even said goodbye.) I knew that I couldn't take anything of value. His family would be coming to clean out his room, and accusations of stealing were common whenever anything got lost. My heart thumped audibly in my chest. I didn't have much time before someone noticed that I was gone, or came in and saw me, and there would be no way to explain. I opened the top drawer of his dresser, and there it was—the spiral-bound three-by-five-inch index cards that Saul had kept in his shirt pocket to scribble his questions and notes of the days' events. I slipped it inside my sleeve, quietly closed the drawer, and squirreled the cards away to my office.

I took my lunch break early that day and sat alone at a Mexican restaurant to read Saul's notes. As I read the scraggly script on each card, I realized that this tiny notebook had become a journal of Saul's disintegrating mind. There were pages of questions about the geography of Iraq, as well as the answers he'd found in the atlas. ("The newspaper is *not* incorrect," he wrote. "Iraq has a Q divorced from its customary U . . . not a misspelling?") He'd recorded what was served for lunch on a random day. The name of his doctor appeared several times, as well as her phone number. I flipped to the next card.

"My girlfriend has a new winter coat. It looks smart on her. Camel wool. Did I buy it for her? Where did I get the money for her coat?"

He was talking about me. I remembered his pleasure when he saw me in the new winter coat that my mother had bought for me at Filene's. It was indeed camel-colored wool, knee-length, and in a plain cut that hadn't gone out of style since the days when Saul was a single man.

"You look swell!" Saul had said the first morning I arrived at the ward wearing it. He reached to me from where he sat at the breakfast table and took my hand in his. "I mean it. That coat looks very smart on you." After lunch that day, he asked me to go for a walk with him. His spine had permanently frozen in the shape of a lowercase *r;* a walk with Saul meant bearing all the weight of him on one of my arms, because he refused to hold a cane, let alone a walker. We moved together at the speed of sap and stopped every few steps to sit down and rest. The nursing home was equipped with dozens of chairs along every wall for just this purpose. During one of our rests, Saul turned to me and said, "I'm very fond of you."

"I'm very fond of you, too," I answered.

When was the last time I'd said something half as kind to my own boyfriend? When was the last time I'd let him touch me while I was sober?

On another note card Saul had written, "How am I going to support my girlfriend? I don't have a job. Does she have a job? I must contact the hospital. Surely they need a physician. I must find work." And then, a few cards later, floating solemnly in the white space:

"What ever happened to my mother?"

I closed the book of index cards and stuffed it into my purse. My eyes stung from fighting back so many tears. I ordered two shots of tequila, which I took the only way one can take tequila, like a fast bullet to the brain. Feeling a little warmth in my belly, I ordered another. "And a chicken fajita," I added, so that I wouldn't look like a degenerate. I tried to drink the third tequila more slowly. Who was this show for? I wondered. The restaurant was empty except for two waiters and me. When I'd eaten enough food to convince myself that I was sober, I went back to work and gave my two-week notice.

On the bus ride home from work, I got off in front of a hotel where the bar had a good happy-hour menu. Free cheese and crackers and four-dollar martinis, which was cheap for Boston at the time. It wasn't the first time I'd stopped at this bar on my way home from work, and it certainly wasn't the first time I had sat alone at a bar and gotten drunk, but never before that day had I acknowledged precisely what I was doing—running away from my feelings—and then righteously, imperiously, said to myself, *So what?*

I would stop at a few more bars that night, drinking alone, realizing, also for the first time, that I didn't have a single friend in my life besides my boyfriend, who didn't drink, and Saul, who was now dead. Later that night I threw up on the train, staining the front of my nice wool coat. I took it off before my stop and left it on the subway floor.

SIX WEEKS LATER, I got a new job teaching English at a small language school in Boston. I wanted to write a collection of short stories, maybe linked stories that I would call a novel. Or perhaps a screenplay about an ESL teacher and her eccentric students. I'd call it *Love as a Second Language.* My plan was to teach classes Monday through Saturday, then devote evenings, weekends, and holidays to writing. Teaching would give me just enough money to pay the bills while I scribbled a salable draft of my masterpiece. It felt like a more legitimate way to make a living than the nursing home. Now if someone at a dinner party asked me what I did, I had an answer that wouldn't make them step back and wince.

After a year and a half of teaching, I'd written only two stories, though I'd started and abandoned many others. I kept all of them hidden in my desk, holding on to the hope that when I died this cache of fiction would be published and my talent posthumously acknowledged, like some hard-drinking Emily Dickinson.

Dave had gotten a low-paying job at a small film-production company in Boston. He was more talented and experienced than anyone in his office understood, living far below his potential. What he needed, it was clear, was to move to New York. Deep down I knew this, and wanted it for him, but I was too selfish to say so and he was too scared to go anywhere without me. The line that demarcated him from me had long ago been erased. I couldn't tell whose fault this was, or what we should do about it. At night I used to whisper into his ear as he slept, hoping to insert myself into his dreams. When we ate together we didn't bother with separate bowls; instead, we hunched over a still-warm pot of macaroni and cheese with one spoon that we passed back and forth.

How do you end something like that? I tried to leave Dave honestly at first, then I went back and tried to make it work. We adopted a dog, we made a 35-mm short film, we accrued thousands of dollars of debt on a shared credit card. I knew it was over, but when I tried to imagine falling asleep without him it felt like being shipwrecked all alone on the moon. Four years after finishing college, I applied to graduate writing programs in the hope that a university could furnish the direction and structure that my life seemed to lack. After several unceremonious rejections, I was offered a place at one school in Manhattan and one in Austin. Texas was a place I'd seen only in movies; it seemed very, very far away. I was so excited by these simple facts that I skimmed over the part of the letter that said I'd get a scholarship and a stipend.

"I'm coming with you," Dave said when I made my decision, his eyes brimming with tears.

"Of course," I answered.

We fought for the entire nineteen-hundred-mile drive from Massachusetts to Texas, and our car broke down three times. For a few days we stopped in New Orleans. It became a spontaneous honeymoon for the wedding that we were always putting off. We went to rock shows and got drunk together and made love as if we meant it. Almost as soon as we got back into the car we started fighting again, tossing all the cruel and tiresome scraps of barbed wire you have left when something is over but you refuse to give it up. Once in Austin, as we were unpacking our collective belongings, I accidentally threw away the ring he had given me to tide me over until we became officially engaged. Later that day, Hurricane Katrina pounded her fists on the city where we had briefly fallen back in love.

In Austin I met other graduate-school writers, people who read and drank as much as I did, including a twenty-two-year-old guy with a Freddie Mercury mustache that he sported as shamelessly as the dark-green girl bike he rode to class. This young man liked to drink, but he liked to go to the movies even more, and in Austin you could do both of those things in the same place, thanks to a local chain of movie theaters called the Alamo Drafthouse. While Dave was making lattes at a miserable coffee chain—the only job he could find in a big college town—I was skipping off to matinees with my new writer friend. Even cross-eyed drunk, this boy was a genius. He could twirl out breathtaking sentences with the speed and flair of a majorette's baton, and this was after eight or nine glasses of Drambuie. Moments before puking, he would offer me a slurry insight into the craft of fiction that was more useful and enduring than anything any teacher has ever said. I didn't want to fall in love with him, but something happened to us in the dark of the movie theater sitting side by side, sometimes the only two people in the audience, our faces awash in the same coil of reflected light, our arms almost touching, then actually touching; then a transmission, a seizure, a curse.

It was just as awful as my mother had said it would be. It was even worse that she was right.

Two writers who drink are about as safe together in the same bed as a can of gasoline and a box of matches. When this boyfriend disappointed me, as any human being inevitably will, I deserted him ruthlessly for another man who drank even more. In less than a month, this replacement man hated me so much that he dumped me and drove across the country with a broken foot. I quickly found a replacement, whom I tortured for the next few weeks. Then I did it all over again with another guy. Then another and another.

Throughout it all, I would call my mother for advice and support. I wanted her to send me care packages with cookies. I wanted her to tell me to forget all these guys and just buy a vibrator. In the screenplay I never wrote about my life, my movie mom strokes my hair and says, "It's okay, Honey. Life is long. And, while relationships don't last forever, I promise you, true love can never die."

That didn't happen. Kathi was disgusted with me. She was angrier than the boyfriends I was backstabbing and throwing away.

"I don't understand how you can just turn your back on people, Nikki," she said. "How did you—how did *my daughter*—ever become so cold?"

(picnic, lightning)

I WAS LIVING ALONE IN AN APARTMENT IN AUSTIN. MY BOYFRIEND of the past eight years had moved to New York. My mother didn't trust me to survive without him, and she didn't trust my new boyfriend, who lived down the street.

"Someone could rape you, attack you, and I'm too far away to help," she said.

I ignored her perverted impulse to protect me *now*, bit my tongue before screaming, *"Too late for that!"*

"Mum, I'm twenty-six. This isn't the first time I've lived on my own."

"I can't stand it," she said. "You're too far away from me. It's different this time. I can't explain it. I hurt. How far away you are—it physically pains me."

What's different, I thought silently, was that she no longer had the money to come to visit. Even if she could find the one credit card that she hadn't maxed out, her addictions kept her more or less housebound. There was no way she could get through airport security with all the syringes and plastic baggies and vials that she would need to survive even a long weekend away from home.

Every time my phone rang, a hot stone rose in my throat, that familiar dilemma felt by everyone who loves a junkie: Please don't be her. Please be her. Please be someone telling me she's dead. Please don't be someone telling me she's dead.

"Honey! I had a dream you died!" she told me.

"Well, I didn't."

"How will I know if something happens to you? You never call me!"

"I called you last night," I said, not mentioning that she had nodded off in the middle of our conversation. I was telling her a funny story when I heard her begin to snore, then cough, then wake herself up.

"No, you didn't. I haven't heard the sound of your voice in weeks. Weeks!"

I could feel the earth shake nineteen hundred miles away. The surface cracked open like an egg and the mucus of her hatred began to spew.

"You think I'm no good," she shrieked. "You think you're so much better than me. I'm a loser! I'm a loser! My own daughter won't call me anymore because she thinks I'm a loser."

I heard the sound of her wailing, then the whack of the phone repeatedly striking a table or countertop. If I was lucky, she would hang up, fall asleep, and call me later, having completely forgotten the previous hour of her life. We'd talk about my dog, a consolation prize for the grandchild I was still refusing to give her. I would try to make her laugh at least once before we hung up, as much for my benefit as for hers. Kathi's joy was like a vitamin that I needed in order to survive and could get from one source only, the unruly crow of her laughter.

Usually she would call back to tell me she was dying. That same old promise I knew she wouldn't keep.

I COMPLETED MY FIRST year of graduate school in Austin with neither success nor disgrace. That summer I'd received a grant that could be spent only on academic study, so I signed up for a writing course being taught by American novelists in St. Petersburg. I decided to bookend my two-week trip to Russia with a few days in Danvers.

"I don't think it's such a good idea for you to go home," my mustachioed boyfriend said to me. "Your mother's a flesh-eating virus. I'm scared for you, baby."

"The flight is much cheaper out of Boston," I said. That was only half the reason.

I MADE IT TO Danvers by the end of June. My mother was waiting for me on the back steps when I pulled into the driveway. She took a last drag from her cigarette, then threw it into the yard. I noticed the trash bags piled up against the side of the house and the scraggly blades of grass sprouting in patches over what could have been a lawn. Mum's arms clamped around me. She squeezed so tight I started to choke. I pulled away and took a good look at her. She was wearing Michael's clothes, a pair of his gray cotton shorts and a big white T-shirt. Either she or Michael had cut off the sleeves, offering a glimpse of her large, sagging breasts. She hadn't bothered to put on a bra, and her sallow skin was covered with scabs. Her once glossy hair was wiry and streaked with white. Pulled back in a rubber band, it reached all the way down her back like the tail of a mangy horse.

"You didn't say anything about how skinny I am."

Kathi reached into her pocket for another cigarette. She had bragged on the phone about all the weight she'd been losing, but I didn't understand what this meant until I saw her a full year later. "I lost fifty pounds!" she said. Which meant that she was still a solid one hundred pounds overweight. Nevertheless, this weight loss was significant to her. And to me as well.

"What happened to your arms?" I asked. There were large, crusty yellow sores on the tops and backs of her wrists, as well as the undersides of her elbows.

"Arthritis." She glared at me. "Not that you care . . ."

I followed her into the house, and she collapsed into a reclining chair facing an enormous television. Oliver the sober drug dealer was gone. He must have realized before the rest of us where Kathi was headed and given up on her. There was a new entourage of drug dealers, skinny junkies younger than me, who came in and out of the house over the next couple of days. My mother tried to introduce me to her new "friends," but I couldn't be bothered to look them in the eye, let alone shake their hands.

"I'm sorry," she said to some strung-out kid in a baseball cap. "My daughter can be very rude." The kid stood there smoking in the squalid room that she insisted on calling her "parlor," then pocketed her cash and left.

Her bracelets and rings were gone, all those diamonds and rubies and sapphires she'd bought off the Home Shopping Network when she was a millionaire. She loved to get good and high, then polish them in a special solution I think she also bought off TV. More than once I'd caught her talking to her jewelry with great affection, the way I sometimes talk to my plants. Now her hands looked wrinkled and naked without ornaments. I saw her finger tattoo for the first time since I was a child.

I knew exactly what had happened, where it all had gone. There was no need to ask. But I did. I wanted to rip off that scab. I wanted to see blood.

"What happened to all your jewelry, Mum?"

"Pawned it. I had to! The fucking IRS. You wouldn't believe what they're putting me through. You would know if you ever called me. Ungrateful cunt . . ." Her voice got low and sleepy. "You never—"

Her head slumped against her shoulder and her body deflated like a scarecrow suddenly released from its post. For a split second I wondered, then hoped, then worried that she had died. A snore, soft and congested, slid out of her slack, open mouth.

No, still alive.

I took the opportunity to survey and silently criticize the state of my mother's home. Not even two years old, this new house was already in the same condition as the old one: trash piled and packed into every room until half of them were rendered uninhabitable. In various spots on the floor, I noticed layers of newspapers soaked with dog urine.

My mother and Michael always had a pair of dogs—one male,

one female, both diseased and poorly trained, an archetypal duo that blatantly reflected their own lives like a fun-house mirror. The dogs, at this point in time, were Lexi and Tyson. Lexi was a miniature Doberman pinscher the size of a medium subway rat. Hyper and intrepid, she liked to crawl up my mother's arm and perch on her shoulder. Kathi had bought Lexi from her sister Penny for sixteen hundred dollars. ("Mum, she's scamming you," I said when I heard about the transaction. "I know, but she obviously needs the money and I need a dog" was my mother's answer.) Tyson was a pit bull, and, like all pit bulls I've personally known, he was muscular enough to tow a cart of bricks and had the brains and the temperament of a marshmallow. Tyson had belonged to a Portuguese mechanic who briefly worked for my mother at the taxi company, until she saw him beat his dog. Kathi fired him on the spot, and threatened to have him deported if he didn't surrender the animal to her.

Of the two dogs, only Tyson was housebroken. Lexi was one of those cute, inbred things you buy at the mall, stripped of even the most basic genetic instincts for self-preservation. Judging by the size and quantity of messes on the floor, I surmised that Tyson was now relieving himself inside, too. What was clear was that, instead of cleaning up the old newspapers, my parents just put new ones down in another spot. I could smell the stench only faintly beneath the stratum of cigarette smoke.

My mother's head snapped up a few minutes later. She didn't seem to see me sitting with her in the living room. She just stared vacantly at the TV. What was on? Some horrible comedy that wasn't the least bit funny. Of all the details in this scene, that's the one I find unbearable, so I've blocked it out. I remember her laughing, hoarse and broken, like a stalled engine. She realized that the cigarette had burned up without her ever taking a drag, lit a new one, and nodded off again. I watched her face anxiously as she slept, something I hadn't done since I was a little girl. Some mornings, and even some nights, I would stand next to my mother as she lay corpselike in bed and watch the movement of her eyeballs beneath their lids. What is Mum looking at? I wondered then. What is she reading in her dreams?

Now, as an adult daughter, I played a game with my mother's unconsciousness instead. How long would her smoldering cigarette hold together in that perfect cylinder? If the ash broke and fell on her before she woke up, I would steal a pill from her bottle; if she woke in time to take the last drag, I would wait for her to offer me one. Either way the game played out, I was guaranteed to win.

"Why are you doing this to yourself?" my boyfriend asked me on the phone that night.

What I couldn't admit to him—or to anyone else, including myself—was that after a full year without seeing her I desperately missed my mother.

Sleeping over at Kathi's house was clearly a bad idea. I had traveler's checks in my suitcase, which would surely get stolen there. I kept my bags at my father's house and spent my days in my mother's parlor, drinking Michael's beer and watching the two of them fade in and out of consciousness. A big event occurred on my second day home. One of Kathi's friends, a boy of twenty-three, had just gotten out of a thirty-day rehab. Instead of going home to see his parents or his ex-girlfriend, this kid came straight to my mother's house. Kathi got on the phone with his mother and promised to take care of him.

"Oh, don't worry, Debbie. He's safe at my house. We're all clean and sober here. I'm making his favorite dinner, my meatballs and sauce. My daughter's home from Texas, too, so we're celebrating. First thing in the morning we're all going to an NA meeting."

This kid—I'll call him Bobby—sat next to me on the couch and crushed up some of my mother's OxyContins on a dinner plate. Soon after snorting it, he went to the bathroom to throw up. I glared at my mother. I couldn't help it. I thought I might throw up, too.

"Don't look at me like that," she said. "Bobby's a good kid, but he's an idiot. Kids like him get out of rehab and they think they can just shoot up like before. That's when they overdose and fucking die, Nikki. I'm saving his life."

She offered me the plate with a little crushed-up Oscar left on it. It was one of those haunting emotional crossroads: do I get high on my righteousness or on my mother's painkillers? The choice was made before I began deliberating. I blew a line up my nose, then lay back and shut my eyes.

ON THE DAY OF my flight, Kathi insisted that she and Michael drive me to the airport. I was amazed when they arrived at my father's house on time.

"We have some very bad news," Mum said as soon as I got into the car. "We're going to lose the house."

I grabbed one of Michael's cigarettes. *Just get me to the airport,* I prayed. *Get me there alive and on time, that's all I ask.* Michael sat silently in the driver's seat, a can of Budweiser between his legs. The car swerved in and out of the lane. Whatever happened to the Navigator? I wondered. Don't ask. Just shut up. If I have to, I can call a cab, a real one, not one of my mother's, and pay for a ride to the airport. I watched all the mile markers and exits on the highway, calculating how much the fare would be if I hopped out now. Simple arithmetic would have to suffice as a coping mechanism until I could get a drink at the airport bar.

"The fucking IRS," Mum hissed. "They have a vendetta against me. I don't know what I did to them." She lit a cigarette and held it dramatically in the air as though posing for a photograph.

"I just don't know what we're going to do unless someone helps us."

EVER SINCE I WAS a little girl I had dreamed of going to Russia—a land, in my imagination, of secrets and snow. Many Americans who grew up during the Cold War were fascinated by the USSR, but I was obsessed. It got so that my classmates and even my teachers at St. Mary's would groan when I walked up to the front of the classroom, a glittery poster board rolled up in my hand, ready to deliver yet another oral presentation on Russia. In elementary school I had a Russian pen pal, a girl my age named Nastya M., arranged by my mother's manicure client who worked for the State Department.

Nastya and I exchanged letters in English, two or three in the course of a year. Although I had been careful not to talk up all the conveniences of my life in a capitalist democracy, I was quite sure that Nastya's letters stopped coming because she had been dragged from the bleak, colorless classroom of her *shkola* and executed by a firing squad in the playground. When we wrote petitions to the priest for Friday Mass at school, I always asked that he pray for those suffering under Gorbachev's regime of silence and oppression. In fourth grade I taught myself to read and write in Cyrillic, using it as a code for the petty secrets I recorded in my diary. *I hate Kristin Cunningham and Nate Leblanc and Mrs. Morris,* I would spell out in strange loopy cursive, each letter hooking up to the next like bulbs in a string of Christmas lights. *I love Ben Chang, but he thinks I'm a dog.* At Andover, I got the chance to learn Russian formally and even won a minor award for reciting a Pushkin poem.

Now the excitement I felt over my trip to Russia was tinged with a childish morbidity. What if an innocent conversation I had with a local was misinterpreted as espionage? What if I was picked up by the secret police, my identity papers stolen, my human rights obliterated? I made photocopies of my passport and visa and gave them to my dad and my boyfriend back in Texas. "Keep them somewhere safe," I said solemnly. "Just in case."

I drank a fifth of Jack Daniel's while I was packing for this big trip, and assumed by an inebriated logic that, because of the latitude, summer in St. Petersburg would be equivalent to autumn in New England. St. Petersburg was in the middle of a heat wave when I arrived. All I'd brought with me were long pants and a couple of sweaters.

I attended classes in a run-down university building that was literally crumbling before our eyes, and stayed in a Soviet-era apartment building where there was no hot water and the power went out at random times every day. Most of the other students in the workshop were wealthy Canadian women who had signed on for a kind of Writers' Fantasy Camp. I tried to say nice things about their stories, but they could tell that I was lying, and when cliques formed—as they always do in summer camp, no matter the age of the campers—I was not a part of them.

The dogwoods were pollinating and their white blossoms blanketed the entire city like snow. After class I trolled the streets in my sweaty clothes, pursued by a nameless panic. Every single decision I made, whether it was what to eat or where to go, felt not only wrong but catastrophic, a turning point that would lead to a path of imminent destruction. If I write at that café, it will be bombed by terrorists. If I take that guided museum tour, I will miss the serendipitous moment that will seed the entire plot of the great American novel I ought to be writing.

The Hermitage, the Summer Palace, the Church of the Spilt Blood—I dragged myself to all these sites but saw none of them. What I noticed, instead, was the homeless veteran of the Chechen War begging on the street, a useless pair of sneakers placed neatly beside him so that he could showcase the rotted stumps where his feet used to be. I peered at hundreds of matryoshka dolls lined up in stalls outside St. Isaac's Cathedral, fat and rosy-cheeked ladies smiling alongside outdated dummies of Ozzy Osbourne and Monica Lewinsky, all of them looking sorry and expectant.

I took blurry pictures of stray dogs searching for food. There were packs of them all over the city, some kind of German shepherd mix. An impressive group of them lived in a park near my flat. One morning I bought a bottle of vodka at the grocery store and decided to follow these dogs down whatever streets they roamed. They led me to a national landmark that I didn't know I was looking for, the childhood home of Vladimir Nabokov. Before the revolution, the Nabokovs lived in a mansion the size of a city block. One wing of it had been preserved and converted into a small museum. The sign on the door said that admission was free for students on Thursdays. It was a Thursday. I thought, Drinking in the morning always pays off.

"*Spasibo, moyi sobachki!*" I called to the dogs loping down the street.

As I entered the building, the heavy front door slipped out of my hand and slammed shut with a loud bang behind me. A docent was seated at a small metal desk near the entrance. She was an old woman with one glass eye and wavy white hair combed neatly into a bun. She looked up from her newspaper and, I think, commented on the slamming door. I picked up the word *door*, at least.

"I'm sorry," I said to her slowly. "My Russian is very bad. I don't understand many words that you speak."

"No, girl. You understand fine," she declared. "Every minute. Every minute, every day, I listen to that door."

She got up from her desk and took me by the arm. Standing upright, she was no more than four and a half feet tall. The feeling of her hand on my arm made my skittish heart beat a little slower; I didn't want her to let go. I listened to her prattling off I don't know what as she led me to each of the exhibits. She showed me the tiny samizdats of *Lolita* and *Pale Fire,* and drawings of butterflies Nabokov had made as a child.

"Thank you," I kept saying. "This is very good. Very big thanks."

When I had seen all the exhibits, the docent pushed me down in a chair in front of an old television set and played a VHS recording of an interview with Nabokov just before he died. The footage was grainy, the way videos get when you dub a copy of a copy, and the audio was warbled from being played so many times. For some reason watching that video unlocked something inside, and I began to weep. I'm not one of those women who cry gracefully. I heave and honk and disgusting liquids spray out of my face. The docent pulled a tissue out of the cuff of her silk blouse and handed it to me, as though she had expected exactly this response to the video and was well prepared for it. I blew my nose, thanked her warmly, and made for the door.

"No, girl," she said. This was followed by a succession of steely, rapid sentences that I couldn't understand. The old woman put her arm around my waist and led me to a staircase cordoned off by a rope and a sign that said, I assumed, NO ENTRY. We walked up the stairs arm in arm, and she continued to tell me things I pretended to understand. "Yes, yes," I said dumbly. *"Konechno."* It was a dark, almost gloomy staircase whose stone steps sloped in the middle from wear. We turned a corner on the second floor, where I stopped and gasped. Above us was a large stained-glass window glittering in the afternoon sun.

"That window!" I cried in Russian. "I know that window!"

It was a somber, beautiful design of blue and purple and turquoise. Nabokov describes it in such loving detail in his memoir *Speak, Memory.* "Grandmother," I said to the docent, because I couldn't remember the polite word for a woman of her age, "I have loved that window before now when I see it. I know that window very well!"

"I know you do." She smiled.

That night I called my mother. "I had such a good day. I met this old woman. She was amazing. You would have loved her."

I could tell by Kathi's voice that she was coming down from a high. She was impatient and irritable and didn't want to hear this.

"It's over, Nikki," she said. "We lost the house. Do you know what this means? We're homeless. I'm going to kill myself. I have everything I need to do it. I can't decide whether I should do it while you're in Russia or wait until you get back. I want to see you one last time."

The next morning, I told my writing teacher and the camp directors that I was leaving the program early. They were shocked but not at all curious about my reason. I managed to get an English-speaking airline agent to change my ticket and spent the next night sleeping in the airport. There was no bar open, and the small cache of Xanax I'd brought with me was long gone. St. Petersburg was in its fabled White Nights, a magical time in the far north full of celebration and romance and long, endless days. From a bank of plastic seats I watched the sky turn from pale pink to bright purple and finally an anxious, lonely blue. It was close to midnight when I squeezed my eyes shut, trying to block out the light.

"Can this please be my emotional bottom?" I wrote in my journal. "All I want is to fall asleep and that miserable sun refuses to set."

———

WHEN I GOT HOME to Danvers, my mother was still alive. Apparently, she hadn't been too suicidal to visit a lawyer. While I was gone, she'd had papers drawn up to transfer her mortgage to me. I listened to her spiel while nursing one of Michael's beers on the parlor couch.

"If you sign this for me, we won't lose the house," she said.

"Mum, I'm so jetlagged and hungover right now. Can I take a nap in your bed?"

"Have an Oscar, Hon. That'll knock the hangover right out of you." She began crushing a fresh pill on her plate. This task seemed to reenergize her and she talked at a faster clip. "I'll pay you the mortgage every month. I'll pay you with interest if you want. So you can start building a little nest egg and buy your own house one day. But you'll have to be the one to make the actual payments to the bank."

"I don't know, Mum—"

"Please," she begged. "You're the only one who can save us."

My choice, my fault. It's how I know that my mother really loved me. In the end, she wanted me to be the protagonist of our story.

I'M IN MY IMMACULATE, air-conditioned apartment in Austin, drinking whiskey from a plastic gallon bottle. My mother is on the phone again, begging me to take over her mortgage. She does this three or four times a day, every day.

"You miserable cunt. You don't love me. You never loved me. I knew it. I always knew it. . . ."

Sometimes I cry, "Please, no, okay, Mum? I'm sorry, I just can't." Sometimes I scream "No!" and hang up.

"How can you do this to me?" my mother howls. She whacks the phone against the wall. "What did I ever do to make you despise me like this?"

Kathi had been asking me for money for a while at this point. I had no right to refuse. When she was a millionaire, I availed myself of her credit card whenever the mood struck. She bought me a brand-new Ford during my senior year in college. It was eventually hauled away for lapsed payments, but still, it wasn't as if I was contributing anything myself. Because of a generous, almost absurd fellowship, I was financially more stable in grad school than ever before, and my mother was on a sharp downward trajectory. I refused to give her cash, but I'd pay something specific, like a phone bill, because then I could control exactly where the money was going. She'd try to pay me back, but every time she did her checks bounced. This was nothing new, either. Even when her business was bringing in truckloads of money, my mother was never very good at accounting. She was a bright, creative businesswoman who could spin straw into gold, but when it came to the practical tasks of running an operation she was helpless. In a few short years, Kathi had transformed a bankrupt suburban taxi operation into a million-dollar small business, yet she was constitutionally incapable of stocking her office with envelopes and stamps or of perusing a monthly bank statement. My mother had bounced checks purely by accident in the past, but she was now doing this with the full knowledge that she had insufficient funds.

"Please stop writing me checks," I'd say to her. "The bank keeps charging me fees when they bounce."

"Jesus Christ, Nikki. I'm fuckin' *sorry*, okay? What was it? A twenty-dollar fee? Is that what you're so upset about?"

Nope. Not even close.

OUR VERY LAST CONVERSATION took place the fall after my trip to Russia. My mother had become convinced that her phones were being tapped. Sometimes she'd hear a little click on the line and would start screaming at the DEA jerk-off she imagined was listening in on our conversation. "Why don't you go fuck your mother?" was her favorite thing to say to them. I thought this was particularly vulgar, and when I said so she snapped.

"What's the matter, Nikki? Is there something you want to tell me?"

"What?"

"You're working on their side, aren't you?"

"What are you talking about?"

This is when my mother accused me of ratting her out to the police.

It was the last insult I could take. Rat was the worst form a human being could take in my mother's eyes. Child molesters, thieves, and junkies were cool, but someone who confessed the truth was the lowest of the low. I remember watching an episode of *The Sopranos* at her house in which a female character on the show begins talking to the FBI. My mother leaned over her chair and spat, literally expectorated, on her own living-room floor, to show her disgust. For my mother to hurl an accusation of that caliber meant that either she had lost all grip on reality or the last atom of respect she had for me had finally split. I think it was a little of both. There were so many things I should have told someone about, but I never said a word, not to my friends or my teachers or even to my therapists. I was so bound to her, so afraid of her, so afraid for her. Maybe I was trying to protect her.

One day I woke up, poured myself a whiskey and coke, and declared to the empty room, "From this moment on, my mother is dead to me." Kathi was nineteen hundred miles away and she didn't know my address. (As I said, bookkeeping had never been her strong suit.) With the support of my boyfriend and a few close friends, I began rejecting her phone calls. It felt like a violent, revolutionary act merely to let the phone ring without answering it. And it rang and rang. All night, all day, sometimes twelve or thirteen times in a row. Kathi left screaming messages so long that they got cut off and she had to call back to continue wailing. She left messages that were more like sound installations of her whacking her phone repeatedly against a hard surface. She would hold her phone up to the radio if it was playing a song we used to like. U2's "With or Without You." Cyndi Lauper's "Time After Time." It was maudlin and pathetic. Agonizing. My mother was acting like a brokenhearted lover. She was worse than any boyfriend I'd ever had, worse than I was at seventeen.

"I can't believe my daughter, my only daughter, would do this to me," she said. "I have nothing to eat. And you won't give me five dollars. Five dollars, Nikki. That's all I'm asking you for. Five fuckin' dollars."

She called to tell me that she was dying. For real this time. She said she was living in a homeless shelter. That her two dogs were going to be put to sleep if I didn't send her some money. All lies, I suspected, and after a little investigation I learned that I was right. It brought no relief. I made myself listen to all her messages. It took almost six months to find the courage to change my phone number. The silence that followed was deafening. It was as though she really were dead.

EXIT INTERVIEW FOR MY MOTHER:

1. Are you mad at me?
2. In fifty words or less, what happened?
3. Was Doris Lessing right—did I *choose* you to be my mother, before I was born?
4. Or did you choose me to be your daughter?
5. If given a choice, and an opportunity to do it all over, would you choose me again?
6. The thought of your death makes me euphoric. Do you understand why?
7. On my eleventh birthday, you told me that you were raped by your cousin when you were my age. Was this disclosure an attempt to: (a) scare me; (b) make me feel sorry for you; (c) have a mother-daughter moment; (d) indirectly acknowledge my past with Uncle Vic, and thereby commiserate; (e) teach me to be strong; (f) teach me to be numb; (g) say, "Happy birthday!"; or (h) all of the above?
8. Is that a stupid question?
9. Every time I make your tomato sauce it comes out too acidic. What am I doing wrong? (No word limit here.)
10. True or false: You wanted to sleep with my boyfriend Steve.

11. True or false: You would have tried to seduce him if you didn't weigh two hundred pounds and thought you had a chance.

12. In fifty words or less, what meaning am I supposed to make of your life and your impending death?

13. In fifty words or less, what do you want me to say at your funeral when you actually die?

14. I'm going to say whatever I want. You won't be there to get mad at me. *Are you mad?* is a childish question. I don't need to ask it, because I will be free. Free! But, still, should I be asking your forgiveness?

15. Do you know how much I love you?

16. Do you know how much I hate you?

17. Do you miss me as much as I miss you?

18. Are you ever going to stop?

NOT FOR YEARS DID I realize what I had done to her.

Like so many times before, I couldn't make sense of the events in my life until I saw them reenacted by someone else on a screen. I was watching a documentary about the mothers of soldiers who had been killed in the Iraq War. Speaking into the microphone, one woman spoke of how much she loved her only child, and how much he loved her. "Every night," this mother said, "every single night, when he went off to bed, my son said to me, 'Thank you, Mom. This was the best day of my life.' "

This kind of gratitude is astounding to me, especially in a teenage boy. There must have been nights when the boy had the flu and fell asleep without saying anything. Maybe even nights when he was sneaking a girl or a beer up to his bedroom and said good night quickly, so as not to get caught. Surely there were nights when he was angry with his mother for some temporary slight, nights when he simply said, "G'night, Mom," and nights when he forgot to do even that.

I do not mean to denigrate this woman, or the form her grief has taken, but I can't ignore the simple fact that she is a mom, and therefore a little bit insane, as every woman who has or will ever raise a child becomes. In the delusion of her pain, this mother was moved to revise her story. Not a lie, really, more of a myth, a little refrain to help her make sense of the world's most incomprehensible despair. Her son was gone—her only child, her baby.

Watching this movie on my computer screen, I saw it clearly— the yowl of a mother who has lost her only cub—and I realized for the first time what I had put my mother through. The worst part is that my mother did not have the finality of death to comfort her.

I was alive.

Home

FOR THREE AND A HALF YEARS, I MAKE TEXAS MY HOME. AUSTIN is a big, sprawling college town full of mellow ex-hippies and well-read misfits, a place where even the most ambitious people mosey along. The sky there is a sunny cartoon blue three hundred days out of the year. Perfect strangers look each other in the eye and smile. The women who ring up my groceries call me "sugar" and "baby." They tell me to "take care," as if they might even mean it.

For three and a half years I do nothing but drink and work, drink and read, drink and fight and love and drink. I can't help it. It's overwhelming—the sunshine, the friendly people, all the abundant life I don't deserve.

So I shut the shades. Double-lock the door. Stay inside for days on end, speaking to no one. You learn a lot about yourself in isolation, like how little you actually need to survive. A big plastic bottle of whiskey, a bag of grass, a bottle of Xanax, some over-the-counter sleeping pills, a pack of cigarettes, a case of Diet Coke, a box of crackers, and a wedge of cheese. As long as there is electricity and plumbing, I can live on this for a week.

That's one half of the story—me in my alcoholic hermitage. The other half of my days in Austin I laze by a swimming pool in a bikini, reading novels in the shade of a palm tree, sipping a whiskey and Coke. I drink alone only if I want to. There's the brilliant young writer with absurd facial hair, who, despite all the deranged and lethal things I said to him the night before, is happy to save me a seat next to him the day after. Then there are our fellows in the graduate writing program. Considered one at a time, we are frail and beautiful children of art; together, we form a race of humans so competitive and insecure that state politicians look Zen by comparison. We meet every night of the week at a circuit of bars known for tacos and cheap beer. Smoking indoors has recently been banned, but no one seems to oblige. If a bar doesn't serve hard liquor, local custom allows us to bring our own as long as we offer the bartender a tip for a cup of ice. (I bring a handle of whiskey that I'm reluctant to share.) After two rounds of drinks, we become a noisy gang of scared little kids shamelessly competing for one another's attention. A conversation about modernism all too quickly devolves into the same old narcissistic tournament—who had the hardest time growing up, who is the most fucked up and/or redeemed now. Nobody ever wins these contests. Why would anyone want to? But I'm just as insecure and competitive as the rest of them, so I play along, screaming obnoxiously as though insufficient volume was the reason I'm not being heard.

Mornings I wake up with a hangover that pales in comparison with my overwhelming sense of dread. Oh God, what did I say last night? Why can't I just learn to keep my mouth shut? Why are my legs all bruised? Where is my other shoe? How did I get home? What the hell happened to me?

I'M IN AWE OF those men whose addictions take them to thrilling, dangerous places—the cold barrel of a gun pressed against their temple, bricks of money stashed in their closet, the threat of incarceration hanging over their head—or those women whose minds disintegrate in a fascinating waltz, the girls who stub cigarettes out on their own skin, walk barefoot into crack houses, grit their teeth in mad bravery while the maniacs sodomize them. Compared with them, mine is a sluggish, vanilla downward spiral. I drink a lot. I cheat on a nice guy with some asshole who doesn't love me. I blab about it to the wrong person, and she uses the information to back-stab me. There's no law against this kind of stuff, no physical danger. All of it neatly falls into the folder marked "melodrama." Everything is fine. I'm what they call "high-functioning." Always a roof over my head, money in my checking account, no one to hurt but myself and a few other people, mostly the boyfriends, but they all signed an invisible waiver the first time we got naked, and so, I tell myself, they're asking for it. On my very worst days I drink alone in a spacious, air-conditioned apartment. I cry and get into fights, a lot of them via email. At some point in the afternoon, I end up facedown on my bed and wake up a few hours later in a puddle of drool. Looking around my room, I try to remember where I am. There is always a brief panic when I realize that I'm not in my mother's house on Eden Glen Avenue. Then where am I?

Seeing the stains on my pillow, scalloped and yellow like clouds of smog, I know exactly where I am. I'm home.

WITHIN A FEW DAY of graduating with a master's in fine arts, I apply for a job cleaning houses. When I talk to Zeke or Carla, which is once a month or less, they ask me why I don't get a better job. Even my boss, a smart suburban entrepreneur, wonders about this.

"Why don't you go back to teaching?" she asks me while reviewing my résumé.

I don't want a career, I assure her. I want to work. All that dust keeps me out of my own head. I love the dull serenity of vacuuming. There's no better way to spend a morning than by attacking the hard-water stains of someone's bathtub. It's a battle I know I can win.

Though the satisfaction of this lasts only so long. Gritting my teeth, scrubbing the checkerboard of shower tiles until my shoulders ache and my eyes get lazy, I start to float away. I'm somewhere else now, reliving it all over again. My aunts and uncles are all around me, my mean teachers. *Her.* I slide down a chute and land in a puddle of dirty water. Everyone who has ever given me so much as a scowl is there, standing dangerously close. Diving into another fantasy, I take a brick to their faces, then carefully mop up all the blood.

"You have no idea how much I love to clean," I tell my boss as she drives me home.

And I'm not lying. I *love* my job. I smoke a joint for breakfast, and as soon as I get home I can drink as much as I want. The next morning my hands shake uncontrollably and a reenactment of Pearl Harbor takes place in my lower intestines, but it doesn't matter. I can clean through my hangover, come home and drink, then do it all over again the next day. It's not such a bad life. Could be a lot worse.

The only problem is that I don't sleep much, and when I do I have horrible nightmares. Some mornings it's hard to shake them off. They cling to my eyes like a gluey caul. A succession of these restless nights makes me loopy and paranoid. Afraid of the sounds coming from the air vents in my bedroom, afraid of the car pulling up outside. Who is it? Is it her? I lean against the door and listen. My neighbor and his son are coming home, talking about dinner, unlocking their door. Okay. I'm okay.

I need to take a shower, but I'm afraid to take off my clothes. Even with the door double-bolted, the windows locked, the shades drawn, it feels too dangerous. For the next three days in a row, there are no houses to clean. My only objective is: *Take a shower.* I write these words in big letters on a piece of paper and tape it to my bathroom mirror. The creature in the reflection is unfamiliar. A monster. Not me. I lean in very close to the mirror. Warm breath, cold glass, clouds fog up and disappear. I scrape the skin on my face with my fingernails as though trying to pull off a mask.

"Ugly bitch, ugly cunt, no-good ugly fucking cunt."

Again I lose contact. An hour and a half passes. There's blood on my fingers. My face is shredded. What happened? Don't look. Cover the mirror with paper, every inch of it, so that it's no longer a mirror. Have a drink and renew the vow to take a shower. Put it in writing again and tape it on the wall above my bed.

It will take another day and a half before it dawns on me to pour a glass of whiskey and put it in the corner of the bathtub, like a carrot on the end of a stick, to lure myself in there.

Life disappears faster than it actually happens. Time becomes a fat and silent beast of prey, something that yawns, masticates, and churns food into waste. A short, miserable span dithering between heart-stopping fear and heart-crushing emptiness. Every day the weather is perfect and every day I drink. Sometimes stuff happens. A simmering tension finally explodes. The man I'm sleeping with is leaving me. Or I'm leaving him. Sometimes it's a man I actually love, sometimes not. Either way, we get into a wicked fight, and for a moment I'm wide awake. Colors come to life, sounds sharpen. I notice every ring swirling in the wood beneath my feet. The dizzying symmetry of a fern. A live oak uprooted in the last storm, lying across the baseball diamond huge and despondent as a corpse slain in battle. The thing he said, so beautiful it hurt. The thing I said, so cruel it was beautiful. The song on the radio howling like a ghost from a forgotten past.

Then, whatever it was is over. Things go back to normal. Life again, or something like it.

Enormous parts of my day are lost inside one memory or another. Certain scenes replay themselves, and I don't know how to make them stop. Sometimes I get so deeply possessed that I forget where I am. I look up to see, to my surprise, that I'm on the number seven bus. I've missed my stop, it was miles ago, and now I have no idea where I am.

What if I lose my whole life like this?

ONE DAY, GORGEOUS AS usual, I'm walking to the store and two short sentences pass through my head: I'm an alcoholic. I need help. I have no idea where these thoughts come from, nor do I really understand what they mean, but I know that they're true.

Later that day, I take the bus to an address I've found online. Alcoholic women meet there every Thursday night to talk about their

drinking. When I show up, I discover that the address is a Thai restaurant. In a room at the back, unknown to diners in the restaurant
or to people on the street outside, thirty ex-drunks sit around a table
and share their stories. The women in Texas are the prettiest in the
country. They know instinctually how to use the sun to their advantage. Even when these women cry, which many of them do, their skin
is so healthy that it seems to glow. I'm jealous enough to kill. Angry
enough to leave. There's a bar across the street—incidentally, my favorite bar in town, the one that reminds me of home.

But a miracle happens, a little wink from the universe that keeps
me in my seat. I was born with a stray dog's instinct to devour free
food whenever I can. Just as my stomach begins to rumble, a woman
with the shiniest hair I've ever seen lays out a platter of spring rolls
and peanut sauce.

"Is this for us?" I ask her.

"Uh-huh," she says. "Help yourself."

I eat one, then two, then three halves of spring rolls and watch as
the other women sip coffee, sparkle, and chat. I'm pretending I've
crashed someone's bridal shower. Why not? Besides me, everyone
here is impeccably dressed. There are finger foods and compliments
for one another's handbags, and a box of tissue in case someone
starts sobbing. All of a sudden the lights dim. Someone lights a can-
dle and a hush unfurls across the darkened room. In the flickering
silence, these women's faces take on a sacred solemnity. The room is
packed, every seat taken, and many more women are standing along
the periphery. It is now officially too late to leave without making a
scene. I reach into my purse, find my pill case, break a Xanax in half,
and gulp it down. The woman with the shiny hair reads from a lam-
inated sheet. This is when I learn about the program of lists, steps,
and promises, the inventory of resentments and personal faults, people who have hurt me, people I have hurt. I fish around for the other
half of that pill.

The Texas beauties each take turns telling their stories. To my
amazement, most of them talk about *gratitude*, how different their
lives are now without alcohol, how hard they've worked and con-

tinue to work so that they never return to their old ways. I'm trying to imagine any of them doing or saying or even witnessing the things I've done, said, and seen. I want to shrivel up and die. I want to go across the street and drink in that grotto bar. I want . . . so much.

Suddenly, it's my turn.

"Hi," I say. "I'm here because I'm twenty-nine years old and I can't remember the last time I went more than a day without drinking. I drink until I black out around five nights a week. I drink as much when I'm happy as when I'm sad. I drink when I'm frustrated, curious, anxious, scared . . . I drink when I'm really just hungry. I drink in the morning, which is considered a low point for some people, though I don't understand why. It's actually the best time of day to drink—nothing bad has happened yet. I drink at lunchtime to get myself ready to write. I drink in the afternoon either to reward myself for a job well done or to console myself for another wasted, unproductive day. I drink at night because it's dark out. I drink all the time, often alone. Here's the strange part—sometimes, I'm not joking, *I drink by accident.* I'll be out walking, ruminating, and suddenly I'll come to, like out of a trance, and find myself at the corner store, in the wine aisle. There is a bottle of Chianti, right in front of me. There it is, in my hand. I'll pretend I'm reading the label, but who am I trying to kid? I don't know anything about wine. All I see is the price tag and the picture. For eighteen bucks, a bird in the silhouette of a gibbous moon. For a bullfighter, only twelve. A castle is $7.99. What's weird is that I didn't even mean to buy booze today. In fact, I swore, when I woke up in the morning, that I wouldn't. Then I end up buying two bottles because they're on sale. Because one is never enough. I go home and finish the first bottle in under an hour, get all sentimental and depressed. I'll try to remember what my mother's voice sounds like. Then I'll remember and open the second bottle and try to forget.

"The worst part, I'm realizing, is that my drinking has nothing to do with her. She's not refilling my glass. I am.

"I always have a hangover. They get worse and worse. I puke so much, if I were a dog, I swear, my owners would have me put to sleep.

Every year, since I can't remember when, I have tried to stop drinking. Just a month, I tell myself. To cleanse my liver. Always the month of February, because it's the shortest. But I never make it for more than a week or two. I can't.

"Now I'm done with all that. It's over. I'm ready to stop."

But I don't say any of that. Not yet.

"Hi" is what I actually say to them. Then tearfully, stupidly, "Um, hi."

For this I get what appears to be a silver poker chip, half a dozen unsolicited phone numbers, and a thunderous round of applause.

FOR ABOUT SIX MONTHS I count and recount the days of my sobriety, one day at a time, just as they tell me to do. (*They* are a grass-roots program of recovering addicts who wish to remain nameless.) My first time around, I'm able to collect enough consecutive days to total one month. For this I am rewarded with the red metallic chip. A whole month without drinking! I'm cured! Just for fun, I decide to abstain for another day, then another week, then two more weeks. After that I go to a bar and order one glass of wine. Just one. One and a half, because I spilled the first glass and so it was only fair to order another. There. I can stop there.

Until the next day. And the next.

I set up all these goals—I'm only going to drink until Thanksgiving, then I'll stop. Christmas comes and goes, and I've been in a blackout for days. But that was the last time, I promise myself. No more. I keep drinking to the end of the year and the beginning of a new one.

In the months that follow, I have two recurring nightmares: my boss tells me that we've been hired to clean my mother's old house. I try to get it done as quickly as I can and get out before she comes home and finds me there. I keep seeing things from our past and wondering if I should try to take them with me or leave them behind.

In the other dream I'm stuck at St. Mary's, sitting in a child-size desk that makes my legs feel huge. Sister Agnes is there, as well as my old classmates. They won't let me leave until I solve these stupid math problems. I keep saying, "But I've got my master's degree! I shouldn't have to do long division anymore."

Fucked up as I am, the insight is inescapable: even in my sleep, I'm repeating the same mistakes.

One Saturday night I go to a coffee shop that shares a building with a vintage clothing store. It's been a couple of days since my last relapse, and this feels like a really long time. I sit in this coffee shop pretending to read, hoping the hours will just disappear so that I can go home and lock the door on another miserable, sober day. Outside the vintage shop there's some kind of party going on. People are drinking free beer and wearing costumes. It isn't Halloween, it's just Austin, a town where a lot of misdirected creativity goes into the simple act of getting drunk. I see this one man with white bandages covering his entire body, like a mummy. He wears a Stetson and a denim jacket and has fake blood leaking out of the place where his mouth should be. When I walk past him, he offers me a beer. "No," I say, trembling, as though I've seen the Devil himself, and run the whole way home.

The next day I say fuck it, drink some whiskey, smoke a joint, and come to the conclusion that I need to quit my job. I'm sick of cleaning urine stains off wealthy people's toilets. My job is the problem. It's driving me to drink. My job and my apartment. I keep locking myself out of my apartment. I've gone through three sets of keys in one month. It's a sign, obviously. Time to leave.

I call my stepmother and sheepishly ask if I can move into the studio on the top floor of her sister's apartment building. I don't have much money, and I'm hoping she can negotiate some kind of deal for me. My stepmother makes a phone call and gets back to me in less than an hour. The apartment is unoccupied, she says, but her sister can't rent it out. There's no fire escape and no heat in the bathroom or kitchen, so the city won't let her have tenants. But I can stay there as long as I don't report her to the Housing Authority.

"It's furnished," Carla says. "It's ready and waiting for you. I'll even clean it up a little if you want."

I ask Carla about my mother. She is reluctant to tell me every-thing she's heard. A few days later, I talk to my father. "She's not in jail yet. So there's that," he says. "How she's managed to escape get-ting locked up I don't know. No one can believe it." According to the mostly reliable network of small-town gossipers, my father reports that neither my mother nor my stepfather has a job. "I don't know where they get the money for, you know, the stuff they need."

"She was always really good at solving that problem," I say bit-terly. *Was.* As though she really were dead.

My sister says she passed my mother going into a pharmacy. "I put my head down, and so did she," she told me. "I don't know if she even recognized me. She looked pretty out of it." My brother tells me that he saw her once, driving around town in a beat-up old Chevy. "Looked like one of the old cabs painted black." She was wearing sunglasses and a baseball cap pulled down over her eyes, slouching low in her seat, my brother reports, like a person on the run.

She's not just hiding from the police. She's hiding from everyone. Danvers is a small town. You can't go around telling people you're a millionaire and then lose it all without having a steamy shovel of schadenfreude flung back in your face.

"Where does she live?" I ask my father.

"I'll find out," he says.

The next time we speak, about a week later, I have to ask him again. This kills me. I don't like saying her name. Even the pronoun *she,* when it refers to my mother, swells into a stone in my throat.

"They're over at Michael's mother's place, that apartment next to the old taxi garage."

I wish I could travel invisibly into her life, observant and untouch-able like a ghost in a Dickens novel. I would be able to check up on her from time to time without her knowing I was there. What would I see? Nothing new. My mother hiding in the back bedroom of her mother-in-law's apartment. All the windows covered up with towels. There were curtains in that room, but they're lacy and white and wouldn't block enough sun, or maybe Michael's mother took them down to protect them from all the cigarette smoke. My mother sits in her bed smoking. Next to her is a small table, every inch of it covered with pill bottles. There are enough bottles of similar size to make a flat surface, and balanced on top is a tea saucer with a spoon and a lighter. In the little drawer is where she keeps her syringes or the empty bottles of methadone, whichever is her dependence at the moment, along with a thick pile of losing scratch tickets. All over the floor, at exactly arm's length from where she sits, are several disposable plastic cups with the remnants of chocolate milk. The floor is littered with dirty paper plates, the plastic wrappers of beef-jerky sticks, and dozens, possibly hundreds, of packs of cigarettes, most of them empty. Facing the bed is a television that is never turned off. In the far corner of the room are a mini fridge and a microwave, the kind of setup you would find in a college dorm. Maybe Michael or a dog is lying next to her on the bed. Maybe she's alone, the light of the television flickering on her—a thing in the shape of a woman, neither alive nor dead.

I get it into my head that if I can know exactly what's happened to her I'll be okay. So I do a very banal thing I've done countless times when I wanted to know more about a person: I Google my mother. It is hilarious and surreal to type her name in the search box.

And there she is, the very first hit. No one else like her in the world.

I had heard from people back home that my mother made the paper a couple of times. Front-page news, I soon learn. Oh, Mum, honestly, I'm a little proud. I read the articles online, about how she lost her house, her taxi business as well as the building it was in, a building described by the journalist as "habitually unkempt." Was the C&A building that bad? Even with the yellow stained walls, I remember it was ten times cleaner and nicer than the house we actually lived in. She and my stepfather were arrested for class-A drug possession; my mother was also charged with disorderly conduct and resisting arrest. She and Michael got pulled over while driving home from a drug run. Mum jumped out of the car and booked it down the highway on foot. When she was apprehended by the police, she kicked and swore.

I hardly breathe as I read this part. I'm playing it like a movie in my mind. What was she wearing? What song was on the radio? Then a gift: in the middle of the article there is a quote from her. The journalist had called her asking for a statement. Kathi's voice comes to life in print.

"Call someone who gives a f——, sweetheart."

Reading this sentence, I miss her more than I ever imagined possible.

TWO WEEKS AFTER I arrive in Danvers, I'm reading the *Boston Sunday Globe* at my father's house. "Look at this," the old man says. He drops a section of the newspaper called Homes in front of me. There are two properties featured on the first page. Above the fold is a house built in 1668. It belonged to a family of Puritans who landed in Massachusetts fourteen years after the first colonists arrived at Plymouth Rock. This house, which has remained in the same family for more than three hundred years, is a beautiful New England saltbox with the original seventeenth-century hinges still creaking open the doors. The first owner, Isaac Goodale, saw his brother murdered by Giles Corey, one of the five men who was crushed to death by heavy stones during the Salem witch trials of 1692. The current owners, I read in the article, are descendants of these same Goodales, now elderly Vermonters too frail to make the trip to the family house on holidays and too prudent to justify the cost of a house that has no use.

It must be a hard sell or it wouldn't be in the paper. The owners acknowledge this in the article and offer an explanation: there are ghosts lingering in the halls. They joke that one needs experience to live in a house like this and not be afraid.

"We're heartbroken to see the house leave the family," they say.

Below the fold is another article, another house, also large, beautiful, and difficult to sell. Or, more accurately, hard to keep inhabited. Unlike the Goodale house, this one has passed through several owners since the original family left. It's a three-thousand-square-foot contemporary cape with a large wraparound porch, offering what the newspaper quaintly describes as "a front seat for the Porter River across the street."

35 Eden Glen Avenue. My mother's house.

"It's cursed," my father says. "That's why no one's buying."

Staring at the paper, I wonder for a moment which house he means.

In the Shadows of a Puritan Graveyard

IF YOU GOT AN OLD PAINT CAN, FILLED IT WITH RUSTY NAILS, THREW in a couple of sweaty jockstraps, and soaked it all in acid rain, then brought this mixture to a boil, somehow burned it, topped it off with toilet water, then boiled it again, you would have a beverage ten times better than the stuff they call coffee around here. I should know, because I'm the one who made it. Having nothing better to do, I volunteered for this job. In a state of desperation, an emotional nadir that I would later come to think of as a *gift,* I wandered into this ramshackle white building and took a seat in one of the eighty metal folding chairs. A woman with thick black hair stood up on the dais. I couldn't glean how old she was, only that her life had obviously been long.

"We need a coffee-maker for Thursday nights," she said in a gruff voice, as though already annoyed. "It is a minimum-three-month commitment. Does anyone want to volunteer?"

I don't know if it was an overachiever's reflex or a deus ex machina, but to say I raised my hand implies an agency that simply wasn't there at the time. Looking around, I guessed about a hundred people were gathered in the small A-frame building, what might, in a simpler time, have been a one-room schoolhouse. Everyone in the hall was either skin-and-bones scrawny or grotesquely obese, and not a single face was smiling. Nor was anyone raising his hand—no one except, I noticed with disembodied amazement, me.

The woman nodded at me and slammed a battered spiral note-book down on the counter next to an industrial samovar. "Write your name and number in there." She walked me through the six-step process for making coffee, pointed out the supply closet, the Styro-foam cups, the cream and sugar. "Make sure the chairs look nice. Not sloppy. In rows of, like, five or six chairs each." She handed me a key to the building. "It's not rocket science, but you'd be smart to get here a little early. If the coffee's not ready at four-thirty sharp, they start to riot."

For no one really knows how long, this building had been dedi-cated to the single purpose of meetinghouse for addicts in various stages of recovery. Situated between a Presbyterian church and the town fire department, it has a graveyard that is close to four hundred years old. Square gray stones poke out of the grass like rows of crooked teeth. Here lyes ye Bodies of the Zachariahs and Abigails, the sea captains, British colonels, and their wives, the "relicts." They were Puritans who looked at the world with shrewd, dry eyes and saw that you could work as hard as an ox all your life, never uttering a nasty word, not even in your dreams, but nothing can guarantee your escape from hell. God-given redemption was limited to a few, and its allotment was random and inscrutable. What's truly amazing about these people was their belief that, given a choice, knowing as all sentient beings do, that you are going to die no matter what, you might as well die trying.

The gravestones are all carved with that curious Puritan hall-mark, a skull gritting his enormous teeth and sprouting thick fronds of grass out of his ears, a bodiless skeleton flying on angel's wings. Sometimes the truth is delivered with artistry. Think of Mahler or Caravaggio or Yeats. Sometimes it's as sublime as stars strung up *just so* across the black night sky. Sometimes it's something as embarrass-ing as a rainbow, or as gross as dog shit on your open-toed shoes. It's a punch in the gut, whatever it is. It physically *hurts*. It has to, or we might intellectualize until we're cross-eyed and blind to the thing we need to see. That's the way it has always worked for me, at least—a gastrointestinal revelation of Truth.

That day, I wandered the graveyard behind the meetinghouse with a cold lump of fear sliding down my throat. I didn't want to be here. I regretted raising my hand. I regretted every single moment of my life leading up to now. Way, way down deep, I still sort of wanted to die. But the morbid little seraph carved into the thin slabs of stone— he was jubilant, on the brink of laughter, ready to sing the eternal good news: Life springs from death, and death from life.

Whether I liked it or not, the person I used to be had to die.

I LIKED TO SAY that I would quit drinking when I got pregnant or when my mother died, whichever came second. As my twenties came to a close, it was becoming clear that I might not live long enough to see my mother go, let alone to take over the official role of being someone else's mother. My friends in recovery tell me that you finally get sober the day before you were supposed to die. It's a dramatic, hysterical, almost superstitious idea, which is precisely why I love it, and why I think it's true.

At the end of my drinking—what I hope is the end—I began to hallucinate. Walking my dog in the early morning, I'd fix my gaze straight ahead, on the flat rectangles of concrete beneath my feet, as though actively trying to shut out the overwhelming nonsense of life in the periphery. I would pay very close attention to the ground, to the wads of gum dotting the sidewalk like malignant black moles, or the impertinence of a tree root breaking through the cement. If I let my eyes scan any higher, I would start to see visions, and though I never thought they were real in any ontological sense, the possibilities they suggested scared me witless.

Beams of headlights on the highway sliced through the mist in two continuous bands of light. The gold light was coming toward me, the red light streaming away. Staring at them, I'd picture a car skidding off the road and pinning my body against a scraggly tree. I could see it all happening frame by frame, feel the air being pressed out of my lungs, feel my ribs being crushed, my heart stopping. Then I'd shake my head and walk home.

Sometimes, as I climbed the staircase to the third floor of my apartment building, I'd feel my foot slip. My body would lean back. Reflexively I always caught myself, but what if I didn't? What if I just let go, fell backward down the stairs? I could hear the hideous thud of my head whacking the steps several times before my neck broke. Gripping the knob of my apartment door, I'd think, Not this time.

Then there was the train. A commuter rail ran from Boston to the suburbs of Cape Ann and cut through my neighborhood every hour. I lived close enough to hear the whistle. To listen for it, and then wonder. How drunk would I have to get first? Blackout drunk. Not hard at all, when auspiciously placed a few feet from the tracks is a decent bar called the Depot. There'd be no way to screw this one up, I thought. No rescue, no miracle surgery, no way to undo it. An action completed as soon as it began.

These death dreams were as real to me as anything I had experienced before. They circled my head like a flock of crows. I didn't especially enjoy them, nor did I feel that I had any power to make them fly away. The best I could do was distract myself. Nature is nothing if not proportional, and the more suicidal I became, the more I got laid. My life had turned into a soft-core porn full of soulless, at times hatefully carnal, fucking. After two months of this, I ended up pulling my groin, something I didn't even know could happen to people outside of construction or professional sports. For five days in a row, I limped to all the various church basements, where *they* kept insisting that alcohol was my problem. I didn't want them to be right, but there were certain facts I couldn't ignore. My hangovers were getting violent. The shakes were no longer a once-in-a-while occurrence but something I planned for every morning. I was physically too small to drink the way I wanted to, and anything less than that was miserably frustrating. I couldn't sustain this habit for long, it had to stop, but for the life of me I couldn't figure out how.

Then one day I found the answer to all my problems. A calm washed over me. I was excited and relieved. Finally, it was going to be okay. I'd just get pregnant. *A baby will keep me sober for nine months at least,* I thought.

It wasn't an original idea. I could hear her voice as though she were standing right next to me: "I quit using everything the moment I found out I was pregnant with you. I just walked away from it all. That's how much I loved you, Nik, even before you were born."

IT IS THE DECLARATION of every thinking woman at some point in her life, a manifesto that crosses all boundaries of class or color or whatever arbitrary thing we try to pretend separates us. It starts out as a girlish whisper, grows louder with each passing year, until that faint promise we traced in the sand becomes a declarative, then an imperative:

I will not become my mother.

It's an ambition born of fear. It's the fear that attends our every ambition. It seems at once inevitable and yet the only thing that we can truly control. Even women who have good mothers, those pillars in the temple of dignity, intelligence, and grace, even *their* daughters find themselves screaming this one sentence out loud, at their girl-friends or sisters:

I will not become my mother.

I will not get fat like her. I will not starve myself. I will not call gin and a handful of peanuts "dinner." I will not bury my libido with the tulip bulbs in the front yard. I will not become a humorless, abstemious prude. I will become neither a cheap nor an expensive whore. I will never cheat on my husband. I will never leave my kids alone with a man I hardly know. I will never get married. I will not deny myself an orgasm. I will never set foot in a church. I will celebrate a devout faith in capital-*G* God. I will never knit. I will learn to hem, darn, patch, and sew my own clothes. I will cook real food, have a healthy dinner on my kitchen table no matter what. I will never hit my children. I will never have children. I will make my own money. I will leave the first time he hits me. My ass will never resemble a large sack of potatoes. My house will be clean and my children will be proud to invite their friends over. I will not obsess over real estate, antiques, collectible dolls, reality television, tarot cards, crossword puzzles, or what the neighbors think. I will never buy things I can't afford. I will allow myself to wear nice clothes. I will dare to enjoy myself. I will not go to prison. I will not become a racist, a homophobe, an anti-Semite, a xenophobe. I will read widely and with an open mind. I will travel the world until no place is unfamiliar. I will never own cats. I will try and try and try even if it kills me. I will never give up. I will not become the woman she was.

I CRAWL BACK TO the meetinghouse I've been visiting for months, with the same thought that everyone else in these rooms has had a million times before.

"This time it will be different."

I cross my arms against my chest as tight as a straitjacket and rock back and forth in the brown metal seat. A woman appears out of nowhere and rubs my back. I'm too numb to thank her. I wasn't even aware that I was shaking. But she seems to understand. And I just keep coming, as they tell me to, though I have no idea why.

I stay sober for a week, then two, then three. The snow retreats, leaving ugly gray islands of ice melting here and there along the roads. The sun lingers in the sky a little bit longer every day. One morning I wake up feeling deliriously happy. I prance around these Twelve-Step meetings telling exaggerated tales of my glory days when I drank in darkened bars and flicked my cigarette butts at joggers. (I only did that once.)

"Look at me now!" I say.

A man named Bert shoots me a knowing smile. He's in his seventies, I'm guessing, an inveterate North Shore clam digger who brags that he never misses a tide. I admire his tan, and the way he can wear a pair of madras shorts without looking supercilious or elderly. At first I think Bert is what they call an old-timer, someone with decades of sobriety hard-forged in the early days of the recovery movement, before the infiltration of softer, gentler self-help rhetoric, back when drunks fresh out of detox were told, "Sit down, shut up, and don't fuckin' drink no matter what." But Bert has been sober for only a couple of years. Not too long ago, he tells me, he was blowing coke off his coffee table with the shades shut, like he was Keith Richards. My God, I think, in another life Bert and I would have fallen in love and probably killed each other.

"How you doing, honey?" he asks me that morning.

"I feel like a million bucks!"

"Don't worry." He laughs. "This, too, shall pass."

"But I feel great."

"Oh, Jesus." Bert shakes his head. "You're on the pink cloud."

It's a temporary euphoria that follows the initial detox. He emphasizes the temporary part.

"Well," I stammer, "what happens after that?"

"You just keep coming, honey."

On day twenty-nine of my sobriety, I wake up feeling wonderful again. The familiar objects in my home startle me with their radiance. Everything has a sharp edge, as though lit from within. A book laid on the table, a vase of dried roses, a vacant chair—it's all a three-dimensional echo of my own potential.

I decide to celebrate by going on a long walk. The color green is making its first shy appearance in the New England landscape. The trees are budding with silky young leaves. Crocuses inch up through the mud. I notice everything as though for the first time. Walking past a cove near my apartment, I see a swan gliding silently across the water. A squirrel dashes into the middle of an empty street, pauses a moment, then scampers to the other side and up a tree. Life is all around me! It's glorious. So glorious I start to cry.

The tears feel good at first—cathartic, the kind of cloudburst that leaves everything clean and new when it's over. I treat this little outpouring of tears like a leg cramp. Just got to walk it off. But I don't stop crying. I can't. Ahead of me are two mothers jogging behind aerodynamic baby strollers. When they hear me gasping, they stop and stare. I blow right past them, tears pouring down my face.

It goes on like this for the next two months. I can see very clearly why so many people who make it to this point give up and start drinking again. Like the rainy season in tropical climates, I am hit by daily torrents of grief, at around ten in the morning and then again at four. I cry and cry, and when I'm done I sleep. Sixteen hours a day, on average. I wear the same pair of sweatpants for weeks. It's miserable. I wouldn't wish this pain on my worst enemy.

That's not true. I would.

I wake up one morning and learn that it's Mother's Day. There's a liquor store forty steps up the street from my apartment. I'm not safe alone, so I call my stepmother and ask if she'll come and get me. The two of us sit on her couch all day, with a bag of potato chips between us. We watch AMC, and what should come on but *Pocketful of Miracles,* starring Bette Davis and Ann-Margret. It's a stupid movie about a stupid girl who is tricked by her selfless mother, a homeless fruit hawker named Apple Annie, into believing that she's not the bastard daughter of a vagabond but a European princess. I stuff my face with potato chips and draft a feminist dissertation in my head. This sentimental comedy of errors is a sick charade. Behind Apple Annie's good intentions is the desire to keep a young girl from crossing over into womanhood by denying her the truth of her past, and therefore of her present.

"Fuck this movie!" I say to Carla. "Pocketful of lies!"

In the climactic scene, Ann-Margret wears a dress that makes her look like a pink frosted cupcake. She is so sweet and gullible and pretty that I want to kick her in the head until she bleeds from the ears.

Bette Davis is looking at her with the incandescent glow of motherly pride. "How can I ever tell her I was never married to her father!" she cries.

A memory rises to the surface—one of those days a million years ago when my mother made me skip school so that I could watch this same movie with her in her big bed. At this very scene, my mother stubbed out her cigarette and said, laughing, "Oh, Apple Annie. You slut!"

I begin to sob. I look over at Carla, who has soaked through a box of tissues. This is pretty typical of her. I've never met anyone as deeply affected by motion pictures as my stepmother. Whether it's a comedy or a drama or even a ninety-second commercial for fabric softener, Carla lets it all come out. It's one of the things I've always loved about her.

I get a roll of toilet paper out of the bathroom and the two of us pass it back and forth until the credits roll. My father comes home and gawks at us.

"Are you two daft?"

"It's a . . . it's a really good movie," I whimper.

I crawl up to my little sister's room and take a nap on her bed. She's away at college, at this moment in time living a life of dignity and maturity while I shuffle around our father's house in pajamas like a teenager with mono. The walls of her bedroom are yellow and orange. Everything else—the curtains, the bedspread, the pretty-girl frills hung here and there—is bright pink. I decide to camp out here for the night, hoping some heliotropic transformation will happen to me in my sleep.

"You okay?" Carla asks me one afternoon. Mother's Day was two weeks ago, and I haven't left her house.

"I tried to wake up but I couldn't," I say with my eyes closed. I had actually unloaded the dishwasher and had ambitions to do some laundry and eventually return to my own apartment. But my legs felt so heavy, my eyes couldn't stay open, and when I got to my sister's bed I collapsed.

"I'm sorry. I just can't wake myself up."

"Don't worry," Carla says gently. "You must need the rest."

"I'm so sorry," I say again.

"You got nothing to apologize for. This is your house, too. It always has been. You can stay here as long as you want."

I mumble a thank-you, then roll over and drift away. It's a little like when I was drinking, and the opposite of it, too. Day and night become the same. My dreams are full of wild animals. They feel very close to the visions of ancient humans, the ones who first connected stars into bodies in the sky. I'm on the brink of something. I can feel it.

—————

I'VE BEEN SLEEPING IN my little sister's bedroom for about a month when my father finally notices me. "What are you doing?" he asks.

"I don't know."

"Why don't you go out and rake the backyard. The lawn needs to aerate before I fertilize it. I'll give you twenty bucks."

While raking the lawn it occurs to me that I have not worked, as in done something to earn money, in months. Thanks to the invention of social-networking websites, I not only know what all my old friends do for a living; I know where they're going for their lunch break on any given afternoon. The people I used to know are now in the middle of their careers. They get up in the morning and put on pants they call slacks. They commute and drink coffee, all without crying or envisioning a train hurtling toward them. They can drink a glass of Cabernet after work and not even finish it. They own houses with spouses, or soon-to-be-spouses. A lot of the people I once knew are having babies. I'm thirty years old, wearing my little sister's sweatpants and a stained T-shirt, raking leaves in my childhood backyard because my dad offered me twenty bucks.

My God, do I want to drink.

That night I complain about this at a meeting. "I'm thirty years old, for Christ's sake. I live in a crappy studio apartment with plastic milk crates stacked up for a bookshelf. I don't own a car. I don't own anything."

A man raises his hand and speaks after me. He says that he is fifty years old and lives in a shelter. After his last relapse, his wife and kids wouldn't have anything to do with him. "I'm looking forward to the day I have a crappy studio apartment with plastic milk crates to hold my books," he said.

After the meeting, I go up to this man to apologize. I offer him my hand, and he pulls me into an enormous bear hug. "Just don't drink, honey," he says. "Just for today."

So I don't. I go back to my dad's house, still afraid to be alone in the rent-free apartment I've just complained about. The next morning, I sublimate my anxieties in a cleaning spree. My stepmother's kitchen sparkles in the sunlight. I clean the downstairs bathroom and the living room and the hallway.

"What are you doing?" my father asks me again.

I'm holding a sponge in my hand, preparing to wash the walls.

"I don't know."

"Want to go for a run with me?"

"Yeah. Okay."

Agreeing to this is proof that I have officially lost my mind. My father is as muscular as he is competitive. In his basement you can find every fitness device ever advertised on a late-night infomercial, which he scavenged from the town dump or, as he refers to it, "the mall." On more than one occasion he has used the word *blimp* as a verb when talking about his daughters. As in, "Don't blimp out like all the other girls in college," or, "Your sister really blimped out this year, didn't she?" When it comes to disciplining one's body, he has very little patience for the process. "So what if it's hard? It's supposed to be hard. Stop whining that it hurts. You're lucky it doesn't hurt more."

Fortunately, my father is recovering from a gruesome shoulder surgery. According to his doctors, he's not supposed to be out running yet, but after six weeks of resting in his recliner he can't take it anymore. This injury has slowed him down a lot, and I can tell that every footfall pains him as much as it does me. For the first and only time in our lives, my father and I run at the same pace.

The next day I'm loafing around the house when again my old man asks me in an incredulous tone what I'm doing. He resembles more the seventeenth-century Puritan settlers of his hometown than the more recent Irish and Italian Catholics who are his actual ancestors. To Zeke, life is toil, and it is a sin to allow oneself any undue affection for this world. My father is appalled by foul language, gift giving, and naps. He refuses to do the wave at baseball games, balks at the very idea of a birthday party, and shakes his head when people talk about sitting down to eat in a restaurant.

"You can eat at home! It's a big waste. . . ."

Which is why it comes as such a shock when this time, instead of putting me to work or getting me to exercise, my father asks me to go out to lunch with him. We drive in silence to a restaurant in Essex called the Village and order a huge plate of fried clams. Even this becomes a competition, as my father and I race to eat as many clams as we can just so the other one can't get them first. I'm losing, but not by much, which my father knows. As I raise a fork to my mouth, he reaches across the table and steals the clam off it.

"So this is where I get it," I say.

"Get what?"

"We eat like refugees, Dad. Have you never noticed that other people let their food digest a little? They breathe between bites. They even talk sometimes."

"Who cares what other people do." He summons the waitress and asks for another basket of bread. I watch with mild disgust as he flirts with her, a fortysomething woman unremarkable in every way. I've seen this before. Men, especially misogynists, always fall a little bit in love with any woman who carries their food on a tray. The waitress giggles and smiles.

"A step *below* prostitution," my mother always said of waitressing. "I'd rather you sell your body than have to touch people's chewed-up food. At least hookers get to lie down sometimes."

The silence returns, and my father and I scan the restaurant for anything to distract us from the unbearable presence of ourselves. Zeke examines the floor, and I keep looking at the bar. Why don't we have anything to talk about? Why is this so painful? Why can't I just relax and enjoy something simple like lunch with my dad without wanting to swill eight Bloody Marys? What's wrong with me?

Then, out of this silence, comes something I still can't believe.

"Remember the last time we ate here?" my dad asks.

"We never ate here," I say. "I never ate here with you."

"Yes, you did. You don't remember? You were in eighth grade. You were very troubled. You were going through that, ah, that hard time."

He was right. We had eaten at the Village once before. After my suicide attempt, when I'd downed a bottle of aspirin at his house, my father took the next day off from work and we came here for lunch. We didn't talk much then, either. We sat just as awkwardly across from each other, trying to look at anything but the person in front of us.

"So it's all over, right? You're okay now?" a younger, blonder Zeke asked the thirteen-year-old me.

"Yeah," I said.

"Okay, good." He knocked his fist twice against the table with the definitive ruling of a judge's gavel.

"You were such a sad little girl," he says now. There's mocking in his voice, and tenderness, too. I shake my head, hardly recognizing this man. "But you've worked like a horse your whole life, and you grew up to be tough. I can't help thinking you got that from me."

"Father of the Year, Dad. I'll get you a trophy."

"Aren't you awful!" He laughs. "You know, I really feel sorry for the man who marries you." He takes the last roll from the bread basket and stuffs it into his mouth. "That is, if you ever get married, which is looking less likely every day."

BY THE END OF my third sober month, the rainy season ends. I wake up and dry my eyes, no longer wondering if and when I'll drink again. A simple thought occurs to me: I don't ever *have* to drink again. Not on the worst days. Not on the best days. And if that feels like too much, all I have to do is stay sober for one day: today. If I'm lucky enough to live until tomorrow, I can figure it out then.

A year passes, a momentous occasion in the sober community. I get a bouquet of foil balloons and a medallion the size of a silver dollar. "Put that medallion on your tongue and if it dissolves, then you can drink again," one woman says to me. "No, no, no," another man corrects her. "It's throw it in the ocean and if it comes back to you, then you can drink."

I hang out with a lot of ex-Catholics and ex-fishermen.

At the end of every meeting, all the alcoholics stand up and pray

together. Holding hands, we break into a weird psychological cheer—
"It works if you work it, and *you're worth it!*" I feel both my hands
being squeezed by the strangers on either side of me. Such explicit
self-confidence is embarrassing to me. But, then again, before all this
I was ready to have some idiot's baby or throw myself in front of a
train. So who am I to judge?

I RESORT TO PRAYER as often as I drank, around the clock all day
long. Sometimes I concentrate my prayers on the people I hate. I
think of the woman I called Auntie Lucy, a creature so malevolently
insane that she made my own mother look like a quaint sitcom character of dysfunction. Deep in meditation, I imagine a white light
growing inside me, radiating compassion for Lucy, a damaged child
of God. I get so spiritual I'm ready to burst with nondenominational
love. Afterward I go out and walk my dog, feeling weightless and
happy. Then, for whatever reason, my brain burps a memory of some
girl I knew in high school, not even my friend but a friend of a friend
named Tanya, how she made fun of my eyebrows once, like thirteen
years ago, and I decide that I won't rest until I track that bitch down
and show her the meaning of the word *pain.*

It's dizzying, all this rage. Disproportionate and insane. I can't sit
still with this throbbing in my veins. Since drinking is not an option,
exercise is the only outlet I have left. I enlist my father as my new
coach, and three times a week we go running together. Zeke's recovery from shoulder surgery outpaces my recovery from drinking, and
in a couple of months he's racing ahead of me, looking back and
shouting, "Come on, Thunder Thighs. Don't wimp out on me now!"
A window into my siblings' childhoods opens up for the first time,
and I realize what it must have been like for them, the athletes I could
never measure up to, to have our father riding their asses before, during, and after every one of their hockey games. Any resentment or
jealousy I felt toward them evaporates in an instant.

I run behind my father uphill, in the rain, in the snow, for longer
and longer distances. I run a half marathon. A month later, the old

man completes a full marathon. "Don't let that hurt your self-esteem, Nik," he says. "I'm an exceptional person, an elite athlete. You really shouldn't compare yourself to someone like me." He rewards our accomplishments of half and full marathons with hill training. I'm in so much physical pain that I want to scream, but, deep down, I love it. That's when I see something I've never seen before in my life: my father in a state of bliss. He loves this pain, too. He loves it even more when it's cold out. It's the only way he can relax. I realize he is a man who would be lost in a bleak abyss if he did not surround himself with conflict, both physical and emotional. He's a runner. So am I.

NOW WHY CAN'T I apply these principles of compassion to my own mother?

Hating Kathi is like begrudging a snake for hissing, a baby for crying, the sun for quietly sinking into the same corner of the sky every night. People are who they are and we cannot change them. It is easier to accept this than it is to fight it. She was sick like me. She did the best that she could.

Except, no. No! I want this to be true, but it's just not working. There is no platitude that can get me over this.

The Lady with the Little Dog

MY FIRST DOG WAS A BLACK NEWFOUNDLAND NAMED GANJA. My mother adopted her from some degenerate hippies she knew in Salem. Ganja's first owners were acolytes in the Church of the Grateful Dead, perpetually stoned and reliably useless. They kept this ninety-pound bear of an animal cooped up day and night in their third-floor apartment. I don't know how my mother convinced them to give the dog up. One day I came home from school and Ganja was sleeping on our living-room couch, like all the animals and people in our life, as though she had always been there.

This dog became the subject of all my elementary poems, stories, and illustrations. I could be elegiac about Ganja at school, when I needed a muse, but, like all muses, it was the Platonic ideal of her that inspired me. In real life, she was too big and lazy to do the frolicking puppy things that looked so attractive on TV. The dog spent most of her life sleeping on the cool cement floor of our garage and, when the weather was nice, swimming in the river, giving her a brackish smell tinged with raw sewage; cuddling with her was out of the question.

Besides, Ganja was my mother's pet, not mine. Every once in a while Kathi would cook an entire meat loaf just for the dog. She loved this animal so much that she paid one of her friends to do a charcoal portrait of her that she hung on the wall. "Is Leah going to do a picture of me after?" I asked.

"Are you kidding?" Mum said plainly. "I don't love you *that* much."

Despite our rivalry, Ganja won my heart the summer day she met my mother's boyfriend Raúl. I was playing in the driveway when Raúl's car pulled up. It must have been shortly after we adopted Ganja, and Raúl hadn't met her yet, because when he saw her strolling out of the garage, he jumped, screeched like a little girl, and ran back to his car.

"There's a bear! Kathi, call 911! There's a bear!"

"What a moron, Ganj," I said, petting her head.

MY FATHER IS A man whose heart falls for a very specific "type"—short, brunette women and medium-sized mutts with black fur and brown-and-white markings. The mothers of his three children fall into the first category, and every single dog he's ever owned falls into the second. The first incarnation of this dog that I personally knew was Woody, a springer spaniel mix who roamed the town of Danvers before the days of leash laws. Several neighborhood housewives and a few restaurant owners knew Woody by name and would leave food for him on the porch or at the back door of their shop when he stopped by on his rounds. My father once passed by the local ice-cream parlor and saw a teenage employee, whom he had never met in his life, giving Woody a dish of vanilla. "I'm not even handsome enough to pull that off," my dad said.

Before he got Woody—before he got me—my father had a mutt named Jagger. This dog was the first animal that was truly *his,* a stepping-stone into manhood who came into Zeke's life two years after his father died and two years before I was born. One morning my father woke up in his apartment on Archer Street and rolled over to find that his dog wasn't there. (My mother was in bed with him; I know, because she's told me her version of the story many times, though my father, who also likes to retell it, intentionally deletes her from it now.) My father lived in a high-traffic neighborhood where an escaped dog would surely get hit by a car. Zeke ran outside, calling Jagger with the dizzy helplessness one feels for a lost pet. He and Kathi drove around looking for him, hanging their heads out the window and yelling his name. The dog was gone. They gave up and went back to their apartment. Just then the phone rang.

"Zeke?" It was Rita Ruta, his girlfriend's mother. "Do you know where your dog is right now?"

It was a question similar to the one she would ask my mother, years later, when in the middle of the night, waking up to find that my mother had gone out and left me alone, I would run next door to my grandmother's house. I ran to her once when my mother was actually asleep in her bed but curled up under the blankets in such a way that I couldn't see her and assumed that she was gone. "Kathi, this is your mother," she would say with a smirk. "Do you know where your daughter is right now?"

Jagger had gotten loose and navigated the five-mile trek from Zeke's apartment to Kathi's mother's house on Eden Glen Avenue. After swimming a few laps in Rita's pool, the dog shook himself off, trotted through the back door into the house and up the stairs to my grandmother's bedroom, jumped onto her bed, lay down next to her, and fell asleep.

"You know what she did then?" Zeke says, his blue eyes crinkled by a boyish grin. "Got up and cooked Jagger liver and onions for breakfast. You should've seen the smile on her face when I came to pick him up. Oh, did your Nonna love to tell that story."

Jagger ran away for good when my mother was eight months pregnant with me. "When you were a baby and you were crying and I didn't know what to do, I would just drive you around in the car and look in people's backyards for him," my mother said. It's a shaky leap of logic, a little psychotic and probably childish, too, but I can't help thinking that Jagger was a harbinger. He was the first creature to elicit parental care from my teenage mother and father, an animal they both adored with innocence, rivalry, and need. Kathi and Zeke have never had a kind word to say about each other, but in Jagger they have been able to come to an agreement. "He was the best dog I've ever met in my life," they've both said many times. And so it is this dog, not me, that is the symbol of their former love. Jagger's disappearance coincided with the two biggest crises of Zeke's and Kathi's young lives: the arrival of their first child and the end of their relationship.

"It's as if he knew you were coming," Mum used to say.

And, like me, Jagger rightly identified Nonna as the alpha female that she was—present, sober, forgiving, and always ready to cook a hearty meal at a moment's notice. I like to imagine her lying in bed with that wet dog and ringing up my father—not yet my father, my mother's boyfriend, her teenage daughter's boyfriend.

ALL THE DOGS I'VE lived with were exceptional in their way, but only one is truly epic. Her name is Zazy. She is part dachshund, part beagle, part something else, or many other things, for sure. Judging by her ability to leap into the air from a solid all-four-on-the-ground stance, I suspect some strain of terrier. Her ears suggest the possibility of Rottweiler in her past, though I cringe to imagine the romantic pairing of a Rottweiler and a dachshund. I can't shake the feeling that there is nobility in her blood, so I did a little research. Nabokov grew up with dachshunds, and Nabokov's mother's dachshund was the grandwiener of Chekhov's dog, which leads me to believe that dachshunds are the chosen breed of literary greatness. I've tried to make a case for Zazy's genetic lineage to the jackal, sidekick of the Egyptian pharaohs, the dogs who attended the likes of Cleopatra in the afterlife, but these theories are usually met by accusations of insanity and megalomania.

Zazy has coarse, shiny black fur with brown eyebrows and cheeks, a white bib of fur on her chest, and white-tipped paws that look as if she's wearing ankle socks. She is not a small dog, but she isn't especially huge, either. The small end of medium is the category I cling to. She was born a stray on the streets of Dorado, Puerto Rico. She and her mother lived in alleyways, surviving on scraps and trash until they found their way to an artist's studio. This man, a wood-carver, made a phone call to an organization called Save a Sato (*sato* is

Puerto Rican slang for street dog). Thus began Zazy's life in the system. She was three months old. Her insides were crawling with parasites from all the rotten food she'd eaten. The organization flew Zazy, her mother, and her surviving siblings to a shelter in Salem, Massachusetts, where they were all dewormed, spayed, and sold to families. The first family to adopt Zazy changed her name to Daisy, according to her files. They kept her for a couple of months and almost certainly beat her. When they decided that they didn't want her anymore, they returned her to the shelter.

Meanwhile, I was living with my college sweetheart in Boston. One Saturday, the day before Father's Day, I got incredibly drunk and announced that I wanted to get a dog. I was overwhelmed with the inexpressible woe that defined my twenties, and I thought a dog would fix me. "Okay," Dave said. He'd trained himself to wait out my impulses, as I usually forgot about them after I sobered up. "Tomorrow," I said. "We're going to get a dog tomorrow." The next morning, I woke up bright and refreshed. I hadn't changed my mind. We drove to the same shelter in Salem from which Woody and Jagger and all my family's dogs have been adopted (except my mother's overweight, neurotic Dalmatian, who came from a breeder). We walked around the cages, considering each one of their baleful yelps, until we came across a cage with a piece of paper taped to the bars. It said CAUTION! THIS DOG IS *NOT* FRIENDLY. DO *NOT* PUT HANDS NEAR CAGE. Like moths to the flame, the two of us pressed our fingers against the bars. With a ferocious roar, the beast inside lunged for us. Its head slammed against the metal bars, and I could feel the warmth of its breath on my hands, which surely would have been shredded by this creature's teeth if it weren't for the cage door between us.

"This one," I said to the woman who worked at the shelter. "I'd like to see what this one's like outside."

What emerged from the cage was not at all what I expected—a shark with fur, a distempered mountain lion crossbred with a weasel—certainly not this skinny, shivering mutt. Her head hung low as though she were ashamed, and her ribs poked through her fur so sharply that we could count each one. We walked her out of the shelter and into the fenced-in yard. She was very suspicious. She didn't seem to like being petted. For the first month that we lived with her she wouldn't look us in the eye. She would carry a mouthful of food from her bowl and hide it behind the couch, hoarding it for later.

She doesn't do that anymore, but she still assaults a bowl of food faster than any other dog I've seen. I regard this as an improvement. Since I was a little kid, I've attacked my food like a stray dog. As a toddler, my mother said, I used to pull out the drawers of our kitchen and climb into them like stair steps to get to the food in the upper cabinets. Once she found me licking peanut butter off a broken glass jar. I don't remember if the jar had fallen or if I'd broken it on purpose, but I can tell you, as a woman in my thirties, that kind of hunger never goes away. When a plate of food is laid before me, my brain shuts down all higher intellectual and motor functions except hand-to-mouth coordination. I will inhale everything before me and not blink or breathe until it's gone.

The one and only time I left Zazy alone with my mother, the dog came dangerously close to overdosing on OxyContin. I was out West visiting my boyfriend's cousins for Christmas. I called every day to check on the dog, but when I called on Christmas Day no one was home. My mother and Michael never left the house in those days, and where would they go on Christmas? I called the taxi company and spoke to the dispatcher, who said the words I never wanted to hear:

"Your mother's at the vet. That dog she's watching ate some of her pills or something."

My boyfriend and I called every animal hospital in Massachusetts trying to find Zazy. My mother refused to answer her cell phone. Once the dog's stomach had been pumped and it was clear that she would live, Kathi's plan, she told me when I got home, was never to let me know what had happened.

"Oh, Nikki, it was awful. We were in the car driving to the hospital and Zazy's little eyes kept shutting. I kept shaking her, and Michael said, 'Don't go to the light, Zazy! Don't go to the light!' "

As soon as I saw my dog, I curled up with her on the floor and held her close, wishing that I could tie us together with a magical knot that only the likes of Daedalus could unravel. "I know exactly how you feel," I whispered to her. "When I was younger, and I thought I would have to live with Kathi forever, I tried to off myself, too."

Anthropomorphism at its worst, I can see this now, but that December I was higher than a rocket on the very pills that had nearly killed my dog, and the mental channel to wild interpretations was pretty wide. Years later, in sobriety and recovering a semblance of human sanity, I know that Zazy's brain is the size of a crab apple— that it is (almost) exclusively confined to one single quadrant within the empirical axes of stimulus and response. However, what this dog and I have in common is a little uncanny, and many, many other dogs and their owners share similar synchronicities. The fact that a unique human life can be reflected, albeit in miniature, through the life of a dog, the fact that our lives ever intersected at all, is not a coincidence to me. It never will be.

"KNUCKLES," MY FATHER CALLS her. "Pound for pound, she's the toughest little dog I've ever met."

Zeke loves his grandpet so much that it makes him insecure, so he does the only thing he knows how to do, and twists his affection into a ruthless competition. "It must kill you, Nik, that your dog loves me so much more than she loves you," he said one day as he lay on his living-room couch and scratched Zazy behind the ears. She rolled over onto her back so he could scratch her stomach. "Oh, that's awful, Zazy, come on. Stop it. You're making your mother feel bad. Would you stop loving me so much? It's embarrassing for her."

My father looked back at me to make sure I was witnessing all this. There was an impish grin on his face. I've worked hard in my adulthood to recover a healthy relationship with my old man. Watching this scene, I thought, If this is as good as it gets between us, I'll consider myself lucky and leave it at that.

Zeke ran his fingers through the folds of fur around Zazy's neck and massaged her throat until her eyes closed dreamily. "Let me ask you a question, Nik," he said, this time not turning around to look at me. I watched him take the suede flaps of her ears between his fingers and knead them gently. "If I'm such a terrible person, why does your dog love me so much?"

I was stunned. When confronted about our violent past, my father will say with all seriousness that he doesn't remember. Robert McNamara, the former secretary of defense, tossed out the same line when asked about his approval of the use of napalm. I used to think it was a political excuse, and a piss-poor one at that, but as I drank and even afterward in total sobriety, there have been times when my own violent episodes evacuated my consciousness in much the same way. Maybe Zeke really doesn't remember punching holes in the wall, or maybe he's ashamed and doesn't want to remember. Right there in the living room, however, the old man was acknowledging this and, in his dense and juvenile way, trying to say that he was sorry.

I'm not sure how you're supposed to respond in these situations. I don't know that I ever will. Again, I have to credit a Higher Power or a clever flickering of neurons—probably both of those things—for the words I found just in time.

"Yeah, Dad, she loves goose shit, dead squirrels, and you."

"That's big of you, Nikki. Really. My God. I never raised you to be the jealous type."

Indeed.

ZAZY IS A CREATURE who seeks comfort after having a nightmare. She has them regularly and, like me, always will, though she has them far less frequently than she used to. There have been times when I was writing at my desk and I'd see her leap from the bed where she was asleep, snarling and snapping at an imaginary enemy. I would approach her as she fought off this invisible monster, and she'd try to attack me, too. It was obvious from the glazed, hallucinatory look in her eyes that she was awake but still dreaming.

("You've had that same look," Dave once said to me.) Then suddenly her face would soften and the hackles in her fur would settle as though an invisible hand had smoothed them out. Awake now, she'd shake it off, turn herself around, and return wearily to her bed.

At night I feel her panting in her sleep. Her paws twitter as she runs toward or away from an image in her dream. Sometimes she wakes me up with her quiet dream-yelp and I watch her ride out the nightmare and break free of it on her own. She is always confused when she first wakes up. As she reenters the world, the light in her eyes is dull and demented. She sniffs the bed, gets a drink of water, and shakes it off. When she returns to the bed, she brings her nose close to my mouth and sniffs the particular fragrance of my breath. Okay, she decides, it's *you*. Satisfied, she turns around and curls up in my arms, pushing herself against my body so that every inch of her spine is touching me. She licks my hands and returns to the even breath of sleep. I don't need to know what she dreams of. It is what everyone dreams of: being helpless, being chased, losing a loved one, getting lost. Relics of her traumatic past mingle with common details of the present day—squirrels and broomsticks, her mother and me.

Just Keep Coming

THE AMERICAN ECONOMY TANKS IN A WAY THAT IS SUSPICIOUSLY similar to the Reagan years of my childhood. Foreclosures and bankruptcies are national news, and in the church basements of my small town someone reports a new drug overdose, suicide, or drunk-driving accident almost every morning. The luckier ones among us are soberly battling cancer, unemployment, and divorce. I consider myself fortunate for simple things like my health and having a steady job. A kind, generous family pays me to hang out with their mentally handicapped son, Jimmy, for twenty hours a week. It's not a glamorous job, but I make enough money doing this to live comfortably without getting into trouble.

Jimmy is a quiet, enchanting forty-year-old. He wears two hooded sweatshirts pulled over his baseball cap and the thickest pair of glasses I've ever seen. Early on, I discover a pretty big overlap in our musical tastes. We both freak out when Prince or the Zombies come on the radio, though any bighearted rock ballad will snap our hands reflexively toward the volume dial. Jimmy won me over the first time we drove down Route 1, and a song came on the radio that made him gasp. For a split second, I was afraid that he had choked on one of the wads of Kleenex he likes to chew on throughout the day. Then he clapped his hands and squealed, "Turn it up, please!"

Music is second only to a sense of smell in its ability to hurtle us out of the present into a past still living in the central stalk of our brains. For me, and apparently for Jimmy, too, the song that does this is Supertramp's "Goodbye Stranger." We barrel down Route 1 toward Boston, past the steak house with the fiberglass Holsteins out front, past the car dealerships with their hysterically waving pennants, past the fake pagoda that failed as a Chinese restaurant and the one down the road from it that survived as a bar—past all the tacky, familiar highway stops we've both known all our lives. The song's tempo builds, and Jimmy rocks faster and faster. "Turn it up, please," he says again and again. I do. The windows of the station wagon are rattling, and people in the cars around us crane their necks to stare. Jimmy shrieks and claps. He rolls down the window, sticks his head out, and howls. I start rocking back and forth, too, singing along. I can't help it. What choice do we have in moments like these except to surrender to joy?

On Mondays I take Jimmy to the movies, and on Tuesdays we try to do something cultural or cardiovascular. I'll drive him to a sculpture garden or a museum, where we walk around for as long as Jimmy is willing to tolerate, a span lasting between ninety seconds and ninety minutes, depending on the day. When the weather is bad or Jimmy's feeling antisocial, we just drive around and listen to music. I have a loop I follow obsessively every morning that passes by Walden Pond.

"Say hi to Mr. Thoreau, Jimmy."

"Hi." He waves without looking out the window.

The nature of Jimmy's handicaps requires slow, incremental transitions between each new experience. For three weeks in a row, we park across the street and cautiously approach Walden Pond; each time, Jimmy spins around and runs back to the car before we can step onto the man-made beach. One day I get him all the way to the trail. We walk for a few minutes before he says, "Take a break, please." This is Jimmy's code for "Bring me home right now." Later in the year, I get Jimmy to follow me halfway around the pond without stopping. It's one of those beautiful autumn days that give New England such a good reputation. The air smells cleaner when nature is in decay. Falling leaves twirl like figure skaters in an eddy of wind. It is just sunny enough for me to love being outside and just cool enough for me to enjoy wearing a light sweater—the most perfect temperature on planet Earth. Red, orange, gold, and blue glitter on the surface of Walden Pond like sloshes of metallic paint. I look back at Jimmy. A wide smile stretches across his face. For the first time in years, maybe ever, I'm completely satisfied with my life just as it is. Watching Jimmy walk intrepidly through the woods feels like a gift that I've worked hard to earn. I'm broke and I'm single, a shameful state of being for an educated American woman of my age, but I have enough money to live simply. I have my sobriety and my health, and every single day I get a little saner.

"Life is good, huh, buddy?" I ask Jimmy.

"Yes," he says as he stares at the molting branches above us.

We get about three-quarters of the way around Walden Pond when Jimmy stops walking. He squats down on the ground, and I hear him grunt. As he stands back up, a trickle of urine soaks through his jeans. I watch as it crawls down his pant legs. Jimmy looks at me with a patient, trusting expression.

"Need some help, please," he says.

For the most part, Jimmy is continent and self-sufficient in the bathroom, though his parents have warned me that he has accidents every once in a while. "Okay, buddy," I tell him. "Let's go home." Since we're already three-quarters of the way around the pond, turning back is pointless. We press forward. A busload of Japanese tourists pass us on the trail. They march past us one by one, and I notice that they're holding their noses. This is when I realize, slowly, as in a dream, that Jimmy has done something more than just wet himself.

I lay some newspaper on the passenger seat of the station wagon and roll down all the windows. We have a twenty-minute drive before

I can get him into the shower. I tally a list of ways I could possibly escape this situation. Isn't there a grown-up who should step in right about now? Someone who is capable of dealing with all this?

Yes, it's me.

THE BUDDHISTS BELIEVE THAT every human life is like an ornament made of glass, something precious, beautiful, and bound to be destroyed. The trick is to see the world as a glass *already* shattered, freeing yourself from a life exhausted in dread of the moment of breaking. It was a lot easier for me to do this in my first year of sobriety, when every new experience had novelty. I got a job, published a couple of stories, had my first boyfriend as a sober woman, then my first sober breakup. I served as the maid of honor in my best friend's wedding. I went to another friend's funeral. Living life on life's terms is what they call it. One day at a time.

But in my second year of sobriety this perfect job starts to get tiring, not to mention embarrassing to explain on dates. In the most selfish and childish way possible, I am jealous of my best friend's marriage. I live in the suburbs with no car, an ambitious paperboy would have a bigger savings account than I do, and there is still no heat in my bathroom or kitchen. One winter morning, I'm wiping deodorant under my arms and the stick is so cold that I scream. A year ago, this studio apartment was a quaint, three-dimensional metaphor for hope and resilience. Now I look around and say, "Another winter in this dump? I can't do it. . . ."

I'm driving Jimmy home to his apartment. I get him into the shower, clean him up, lay out fresh clothes for him to put on in whatever order makes sense to him. Sock, sweatshirt, sweatshirt, another sock, then underpants. . . . When it's all done, he asks to go to Dunkin' Donuts. I order him a coffee with cream and sugar. Like a priest performing a rite, he takes one sip, then pours the coffee into the trash. Right now it is early twilight, a short lapse that cinematographers refer to as "the magic hour." The sky was a flood of gold pouring over a cliff of blue-gray clouds. These colors, this exact quality of light, are enough to make me drink.

NOT LONG BEFORE I changed my number and silenced her for good, my mother left me a voice mail that was stranger than any other. She wasn't crying or screaming or banging the phone against the table. Her voice sounded even, almost calm. "I don't know why you won't talk to me, Nikki," she said. "Maybe you're writing a book about me, that's why. Well, good luck."

I deleted the message, stomped my foot in childish rage, then pulled a long, hard swig from the plastic bottle of whiskey I always kept close by. "I would *never* write about you," I whispered, as though, two thousand miles away, she might hear me.

The truth was, I wrote about her all the time in my fiction. She was a quadriplegic housewife torturing her family from her wheel-chair. She was the schizophrenic shut-in who talked to the fisher cat outside her window. "These characters aren't sympathetic enough," the people in my writing workshops said. "I don't believe these char-acters are real," one classmate asserted. "I mean, poor people don't talk like this."

It's an axiom of writing workshops that if a gun is introduced at the beginning of a story, it has to fire at the end. Following that pre-scription, if the protagonist is shooting up in the opening scenes, he or she has only two fictional destinies: to get clean or to die. "If you write about morally compromised people," one of my teachers stressed, "they *have to* make the choice to get better. Otherwise there's no *redemption*." In movies, transformation like this happens in a mechanical blink of the eye. Gaping flesh wounds are healed in the space of a song. A war is won, a baby is born, and all the blood is cleaned up during the invisible cut between scenes. Everything has a beginning, a middle, and an end, and after a climax there is always an epiphany and a resolution. It sounds lovely and sometimes it's even true, but not for us. My family does not magically repair itself.

We hurt one another and make feeble amends and just go on torturing ourselves for years without musical accompaniment. My father
and Carla separate. Neither has the money for a divorce. They are
bound legally by a mortgage and the worst home-selling market the
country has ever seen. For them, my brother and sister, even the family dogs, it all gets about as ugly as these things can get. My mother
does not get sober. From what I hear, her hair has turned completely
white and she relies on a portable oxygen tank to breathe. Just a few
miles away from where we used to live, she is gasping her way through
another twenty-four hours.

While a few things change, much remains the same. I used to be a
miserable, spiritless, insecure egomaniac who smelled like whiskey.
Now I am a well-intentioned, sometimes volatile, even more insecure
egomaniac who smells like coffee. My friends in the recovery movement tell me that's just fine for now.

"Progress, not perfection," they say.

"You know, I really hate all the sententious crap you people spew
out," I answer. "It makes me feel like a member of a brainless cult."

"That's okay, honey. You just keep coming."

JIMMY AND I DRIVE past two liquor stores and five restaurants that
serve beer and wine. I make a note of each and every one. But I don't
drink that day, or the next day, or the next, because one thing has
changed dramatically: I no longer have any excuses.

IN SOBRIETY, MEMORIES RETURN slowly and in the wrong order.
Often there's no trigger, just a rumble in my stomach or a fluttering
in the rib cage, like a small animal is trapped inside and wants to find
its way out. Pieces of dialogue, images, entire scenes sometimes spill
out unexpectedly, then slither into the grass. I try to catch them, to
see what more they have to say, only to watch them slip between my
fingers. Pinning down a memory is like gathering a handful of water
and trying to hold on. In the end, it's an act you can only mime.

Something my mother said pops into my head one day. It was years ago, when she was trying to recover from her own resentments.

"Write me a letter, Honey."

But I have so much to say to you. How could I explain? How would I even begin?

"Say a prayer, get a pen and a notebook, and just see what happens," my sober friends tell me. So that's what I do. I start to write about that day, a lifetime ago, when Mum and I went and smashed the windshield of some woman's car.

ACKNOWLEDGMENTS

Brian McGreevy, *il mio migliore fabbro,* love and thanks without end.

Lydia Wills and Celina Spiegel, your faith and guidance have been the biggest gift. Hana Landes and Nora Spiegel, your patience and hard work are invaluable.

Writers' residencies and fellowships have made it possible for me to write this book. Profound thanks to the generosity of: the Michener Center for Writers; the Keene Foundation; the Blue Mountain Center (best colony ever), Jentel; Yaddo; Hedgebrook; MacDowell; and Guili Pecci.

My mother and father are exceptional beings who will always fill me with gratitude and love. I feel so lucky to have had two extra parents, My Wicked Stepmother and Michael. Thank you, Paul and Elyse, the very best partners in crime and virtue; Jason—I could write a whole book about you alone.

Without the love and support of the following people, I would not be able to breathe let alone write: David Andalman, no limit soldier, I am indebted to you for life; Ellie Egan, tall, brilliant, beautiful, and generous; Chelsee Shiels and the Lowes, who really ought to be listed in the family section; Barb B. and Barb W., for love and chocolate; everyone at the Danvers Eye Opener and the White Whale; Joe and John Ahern; Rev. Beckie Hickok; Missy McCutcheon and Birdie; Nate Rostron and Paige Normand, who read ugly first drafts yet offered life-sustaining encouragement; Duff Hildreth; Adam Gardner; all the people in and out of the rooms who prayed for me, you know who you are; last, first, always and forever—Zazy.

DOMENICA RUTA was born and raised in Danvers, Massachusetts. She is a graduate of Oberlin College and holds an MFA from the Michener Center for Writers at the University of Texas at Austin. She was a finalist for the Keene Prize for Literature and has been awarded residencies at Yaddo, MacDowell, Blue Mountain Center, Jentel, and Hedgebrook.

A B O U T   T H E   T Y P E

This book was set in Sabon, a typeface designed by the well-known German typographer Jan Tschichold (1902–74). Sabon's design is based upon the original letter forms of Claude Garamond and was created specifically to be used for three sources: foundry type for hand composition, Linotype, and Monotype. Tschichold named his typeface for the famous Frankfurt typefounder Jacques Sabon, who died in 1580.